The Chapbooks:
Collected Poems

The Chapbooks:
Collected Poems

Phil Linz

ANOINTED ROSE PRESS™ PUBLISHING
Upper Darby, Pennsylvania

The Chapbooks: Collected Poems

Copyright © 2019 by Phil Linz

Email: linzp18@verizon.net

ISBN-13: 978-0-9896110-5-3
ISBN-10: 0-9896110-5-1

Anointed Rose Press, Publishers
Upper Darby, PA 19082
Email: septembersummer09@gmail.com

Library of Congress Control Number: 2019913653
Library of Congress Catalog-in-Publication Data

The Chapbooks: Collected Poems/Phil Linz
p.cm.

ISBN (trade pbk.: alk. Paper)

25 24 23 22 21 20 19   AnR LS   1 2 3 4 5

1.Poetry (Poetic Works by One Author   2. Interpersonal Relations

Cover Design/Editor:
ANOINTED ROSE PRESS/September Summer
Upper Darby, PA (484) 378-0939

Illustrations: Ryn Gargulinski

ANOINTED ROSE PRESS™

The Anointed Rose Press name and logo are registered Trademarks of ANOINTED ROSE PRESS™ PUBLISHING

Dedication

For Jack Kerouac, Allen Ginsberg, and William S. Burroughs;

for Bill Wilson and Dr. Bob Smith;

and for Stan Dale and Ram Dass

Table of Contents

from **The Holiday Poems: 1986 - 2005 (2002; Second Edition, 2006)**

from ***David's Book (2007)***

from *Ilene's Book: Poems and Photographs (2008)*

Acknowledgements

Poems have appeared, possibly in slightly modified form, in the following magazines and books:
Borderline Personalities: Poetry from Rowe, Enlighten Journal, The Harte Beat, Out-Sight, Vice, Cosmetiscope, Recovery Network Program, Phelps Hospice Newsletter, And Now For Something Completely Different, The True Wheel, HAI Lights, Medicinal Purposes, Touching Body and Spirit, Scarborough Presbyterian Church Newsletter, Erato; **Poems: 1970's - 1990's**, (privately printed, 1994), **Lunch With The Muse** *(Petit Pois Press, Brooklyn, NY, 2001), and* **The Company We Keep** *(Poet Warrior Productions, Wayne, NJ, 2003),*

Several poems have appeared on the following websites but may not be currently available:
https://foxchasereview.wordpress.com/the-fox-chase-review-winter-201
www.hai.org.ws
www.angelfire. com/journal/saadaya.
https://dansemacabreonline.wixsite.com/neudm
https://jerryjazzmusician.com/2019/09/since-1970-a-poem-by-phil-linz/

Illustrations (Kyzen) © 2005, 2019 *by Ryn Gargulinski*

Photographs courtesy Linz Family Archives.

Fierce Grace Press
c/o Phil Linz
7 Rockford Road, Unit B-8
Wilmington, DE 19806

linzp18@verizon.net

Introduction: What This One's About

*"I just want to have a book with all the
poems in it before I die."*
--from Joel Oppenheimer,
***Village Voice**, circa 1969*

Each chapbook had its own theme--family, friends, the dirty XXX stuff of the first,
But each remains a part of who I am, who I might want to become:
A poet. A brother, a son, a friend. A sexual being. An addict. A man.
Even though some work might offend; it's *"not for everybody,"* (from **Steppenwolf**, long ago).

Parts of me some would want me to hide; I've done enough of that, this life;
Instead, here's (close to) the all of me. Been writing since college, '71, a lifetime of words;
Wrote of hospice & holidays, of friends, family, teachings, learnings,
Tried hard to write truth. Personal, subjective; my own, limited truth.

But real--real as I could make it. Finally, unapologetic,
Here are the words, the books; the poetry. Here's my truth.
I'm an old man now, 65; maybe the poems will die with me (page 276**)**,
But I've made this book, I own its truth; it's what I've done, it's what I am.

I put it out into the world, it's yours now, I can own it & let it go simultaneously.
Ten chapbooks of poetry. One book, to stand on its own. The verse I may yet contribute.

Wilmington, DE
November 2018

THE
SEX
STUFF

"It is because our hearts live in our bodies
That we choose such twisted pathways to Love."

- PL, January 97

Author's Note

In the fall of 1996, I noticed that some of my poetry had taken a somewhat pornographic turn (Stripper Fantasy, Phone Sex Poem, Zipless); it was interesting to me, because I'd never explored that area of writing much before. Just like most members of XX Century American Culture, I'm constantly awash in images of sexuality, from the erotic to the pornographic - occasionally even touching on the sweetness we've come to call Love (though few, certainly including myself, have any idea what that truly is). The idea for a chapbook then came to me, with the prevailing idea being an exploration of sexual themes. The poems in this book date back to one of my favorite poems, which unfortunately describes an extremely painful time for both a friend (whom I hurt very deeply) and myself. You'll note that there are approximately as many poems written for male lovers as for female ones; it's my belief that we're all given blessings and curses, burdens and gifts. Though I make no claim to understand the glorious complexities of my own desires, I know that my own sexuality has always, in this lifetime, been expressed with both men and women. The pendulum swings as it will. Some parts of our lives are given to us: choice is only an illusion in these cases.

The last poem was written in an attempt to sum up the book and my thinking, here, now. I know absolutely that all will change: body, desire, even spirit (in form, if not in essence). We are all works-in-progress; we start where we are: here; now. Sexuality's a gift, sometimes a burden; Rilke said, "*Live* the questions now." I do. I believe we're all doing just that.

In Love,

PL, Rahway NJ
January 97

5.

(7) Poem: for Carol

They're walking on hot coals in Beverly Hills, but
Yuppie-*siddhis* don't impress me much

But the sleepwalker, in dream state
Thinking they were honey-covered scoops of ice cream
Laughing, placed those burning coals on his lover's breasts

Vicious, ignorant scars
The horrors of his own hand
Appear to him on waking:
"What has been done, cannot be undone."

So much cruelty in the name of love
So much pain in the guise of protection
So much selfishness returning to loneliness

Her deafening silence (her anger just)
The ordinary ring of a telephone

NYC
March 86

7.

(8) Holiday

Time is illusion.   Track lighting, Tina Turner, lusting for the legs
       of the long-haired Chinese boy, burning in the silent
       tease of ripped faded jeans.

He is unsmiling, unseeing, sharing late dinner with his
       unshaven friend. Apart, I am ghost, sipping coffee.

Beyond brittle glass, no relief: the moving crowds.

Earlier, lit with neon and classics, I find the teacher's
       first book, find a poem on walking late in the Village,
       as I too walk late, the same Village

Lust versus friendship: desires becoming needs. The bastard
       Time, always all-powerful. Bitterly accepting: waiting.

Her dress: a tight-fitting return to op art, tightest at her tiny waist;
       I note the moves of her wide hips, she exits, I still stare

Her butt
His hair
My words

"The way through is given by accepting the now."

The Village night: another.

NYC
August - October 87

(9) Poem for Leslie: On the New Beginning

It seems to be that now you've learned this new thing, this your given,
      this your own: nova-bright, searingly sweet, ecstatically real
It seems that now the past is only as a mildness, an insignificance
      against these resplendent fires, these torrents of relaxation

I am not sorcerer, not magician, only caring, loving man, slowly learning the rules
      of your body, slowly discovering new pathways to that hidden wellspring,
      that love-sweetened center;

I knew of the power that lives within, prayed you would know its rise,
      prayed it would make you sing, scream, surrender—
Prayed that you would know such deserved passion.

Only the barest opening of the door. This path toward a knowledge, not of words
      but of growth and feeling, of experience and life, is now before you:
Only a beginning, but, truly, a recognition, of the joy and power and spirit of woman.
      Claim it now, own it: now it is yours; now it belongs to you.

NYC - NJ
August 88

9.

(10) Prosepoem: for L.

A fragment, from an ancient manuscript:

"And at this time, in the course of his wanderings, the seeker found himself in the middle of a large city. The city was situated near the dark waters, which are thought to be holy and life-giving by some; it gave the traveler calm, knowing that he was near the sacred places.

"In this city, as was his habit, he joined with others who believed as he did. He found shelter, and work, and went about his life quietly, knowing, at all times, that he was on his own particular journey of the inner and outer spaces and was, in many ways, only passing through: in this city, in this time, among these people. However, as often happens, he met with a woman; better, it was at the proper time, that a woman found him. With surprising rapidity, they were soon joined together, physically, mentally, and spiritually; they shared great pleasures as each helped the other to grow in these several areas. In time, each learned to take from the other, each learned to give to the other; slowly, each came to an understanding of the other's spirit, as well as learning more fully of their own.

"There were times in their lives that the couple separated, one from the other, in order for each to do their own, necessary work. It was even said that both, in time, found other loves, other spouses; it was common knowledge, for example, that the children which came from his seed, the children which grew in her belly, were not the result of this special union. Both knew that they were living their lives as their lives must be lived, that the deepest is not always the wisest, and that many of our choices are not, finally, our own. This man, and this woman, lived their lives, and died, as we all must die; in as little as three generations, a very short time, really, their lives, and the stories of their lives, were all but lost, save by the storyteller, save by the one who listens well and catches meaning in things, save by your humble servant, who knows that the life-force of these two exist in some, in this generation, and will exist in some, a thousand years hence: when man and woman join, and move beyond the body and the mind and embrace the spirit in each other—it is then that these ancients are reborn and live again, loving and sharing again and again and again."

Nothing further from this unknown writer has even been found.

NYC -NJ
December 88

(11) Moods: for Corso

When April feels like winter, I walk the evening streets, the city streets, my city streets,
Feeling neither separate nor together, unsure of the machinations of my own feelings,
But feeling. I've not doubt that I'm now feeling.

She's gone. She still calls; I live my refrain,
        "Just friends, lovers no more - "

My actions, my choice. Aware, I sent her away:
Expecting; not believing. The grayness which follows relief. Where I am, now.

I walk the April winter streets to the place of the poet, surrounded by those who will follow,
        "who know me not nor care me less;"

Breathe.
Again.
(Repeat.)

Living states of selfish pain, self-created fear, self-twisted anger, self-protecting
        attacks on the Self:
Illusion. Living the illusion.

NYC
April - July 89

(12) Poem: for Cheryl

Anticipation: the disappointment

Realization: the unattainable

NYC
June - August 89

(13) Poem for Anthony: The First Night

Anxiety, reflected in opposites:
The ride. Nervous smiles, barely-controlled lust: hope, nothing more.
Protected by East Village walls, the doubly-desired embrace:
After that, the understood; the natural. The absolutely wonderful.

The dance of loving brothers, the blonde youth, the dark man,
Learning through givings, strokings, through hot tongues fiercely mating,
Knowing through tightnesses, passions, strength, through joy;
His seed upon me, mine protected, hotly, within.

More than one brilliant night, more than typical passing of strangers,
Letting the road rise before us. A new loving friendship, as it begins.

NYC - NJ
July 90

(14) "Loving Yvonne"

Invisible the sweetness,

    the trembling, the hot damp flesh;

      Spring; early.

           NJ - NYC
           April 91

(15) Poem of the Second Chakra

They read me, quite sure they even smell me,
Know too well the hunger dripping through pores;
The easy small talk, the relaxed, teasing air;
Lies, of course. Truth the blinding need, for touch, contact: for human resolution.

Odd this life, mind pretending direction, other, well-known forces leading me on,
Old actions, dimly lighted spas, lusts emptily assuaged; sad; acceptable
Women in wide weekend beds, breasts, bellies, the holy living ***MAGIC!*** within,
The street: gorgeous, potential: polite, definitive "No." Anger rises; tension high.

To give up desire, to lose this sparking, delight-filled suffering,
Available now, techniques and teachers, the many ways toward truth.
My heart, my loins! The tightly-loving clasp, woman, man!
Such dreams own me, today. And if all's illusion, still, the pursuit! As if it mattered!

Left hand on the phone, right at my crotch: pathetic, these fantasies live fully, in me;
Knowledge, will to change: not enough. The wondrous power of the second place.

NYC
March 95

15.

(16) The First Touch of Your Lips
for Ken

The first touch of your lips:
The way of beginning. Before, only prologue, smiles, internal possibilities;
Now we were sure; now questions unnecessary.   The simple request; the cab ride.
Close, the tender act: holding hands. Crosstown.

And O! Your lips! Full, warm, giving, wanting,
Truly a match for my own, tender on shoulders, cheeks, the hollows of the ears, the neck,
Pressing tightly, warm against their mate, the heat of our mouths, the heat within us;
And quietly, in assent, to my cool narrow bed.

The lovings of that bed, the gentle, persistent pleasures,
Kissings of arms, of bellies and eyes, savoring warm smoothness, the lovely skin,
Your hard strokes against me, my hard pressings at your groin, at your thigh,
Like a dreamy youth, trusting, you sleep in my arms.

We seek our special ones. I seek nights like this, pleasures repeated, but more:
Partnership, warmth, shared intimacies: this night a holy gift. Yet: I dream of more.

NYC
May - August 95

16.

(17) Stripper Fantasy
for Betty

"And now, without further introduction: here's Betty!"

Tired applause, the band giving a hot walking blues,
You enter, the spotlight hits your smile, your tight silver gown,
Strutting the runway, owning the stage, that clear, knowing smile,
Giving us this pleasure; doing the work you were meant to do.

Smiling, moving, thrusting your hips, proud of your firm slim body,
Slowly the zipper in the back, moving that sweet butt side to side,
The silver falls slowly past the hips, revealing your back, shapely, sexy;
Red bodysuit, black stockings & garters, black lace at your crotch; and your smile.

Humping the curtain now, driving men wild, lust rising in the overheated room,
The prop of the chair, slow dark nylons removed over holy white thigh,
Your back again to the now-screaming crowd, the red lace unbuttoned, removed,
Turning, facing your thousand would-be lovers, caressing yourself, as in a dream;

Two curtain calls, your high excitement, your lover waiting in the wings;
And only I pull down your panties, only my mouth moves to your gorgeous cock,
        the stand-in for all who'd love you, still shouting, still screaming your name.

NYC
February 96

17.

(18) Phone Sex Poem

for Michael, among others

This city of searching strangers; the line. *"What'cha looking for tonight?*
Agreement; acceptance. The seven-digit connection; the quick hang-up.

Naked, alone: my dark bed. The plastic receiver in my left hand,
My rising cock in my right. Hearing your voice,
"If I were next to you," and because I want you, you are;
Lying above me, kissing my neck, my lips, my left nipple, my right—

AHHHH! - my body given over to your control, I'm aching to please you,
Stroking chest, belly, thighs, your living cock pressing hard on mine,
Rising, your slow dance, my hungry lips, playful, teasing,
My mouth to the swelling head, my tongue loving the shaft: you, entering me.

Filling my mouth with your power & beauty, fucking my mouth as
Man fucks man, taking your pleasure, giving me mine; gently, you withdraw;
Our hands agents of joy, our lips pressing each other, again, again,
And now, as you would have't: I straddle you, you enter me; in mutual desire.

Your cock hard against tight inner folds, whimpering, past sphincter, into me,
Whimpering, but wanting, wanting more, wanting your man-strength deep within me,
All the way, hot loving man fucking me hard & deep; becoming youth, becoming pussy,
Becoming the man I'm meant to be. Dreaming glorious pressures: the distant spasms.

The deep breathing, the moments after orgasm, for you, for me.
And no, I guess we won't meet. *"But it was very nice."* *"Yes—for me, too."*

The silence after the hang-up; still naked, still alone, my dark bed;
Wipe the lust-cream from belly & arms. Sigh. Dream of the man:

Whose voice just loved you.

NYC
February - March 96

18.

(19) Poem of Pursuit
for Michael

The only long conversation, the café, late, weeks ago,
You claiming the negative to my positive, a human battery being formed,
Dream of us lying on the floor, almost touching: your poetry, mine, even ours;
Telling you, at the random street meeting, of the odd new dream: being shat upon.

All of this mere mind stuff, with large reserves of sweet lust-thoughts.
Can't, even won't, guess your mind. Mine's moving fast enough for both of us.
The necessary first: your smiling agreement. The apartment: the first real embrace.
The natural, slow progression. Our lips, our skins, our creation: joy. And more.

Plans keep screwing up; mine, anyway. Dinner went well Saturday, gifts, a new poem,
Planned to party in Queens, tired, blew that off. Intended nap, then late visit,
Slept; phone. Horny closeted drag queen, gave service, pleasure; but saved myself.
Slept *"just a bit more."* Woke 4:30…blew it again! Dream, again. Of not-tonight.

Confused by strength of desire, by fumbled efforts, bad timing, by your intricate mind:
In the midst of the familiar, disorienting field: I wait. I want. I pursue.

NYC
May 96

(20) Hallway Poem
for MJ

"When one door closes, another opens;
but it's hell in the hallway."

A message on the machine: *"…it's shit, is what it is."*
Later, the chance meeting, dawn on Avenue A. The end of your day,
The beginning of mine. Neither satisfied, this bright clear morning:
A call for hope, for optimism. The embrace genuine, warm; brief. We move on.

Still in pursuit: the odd "date," last week. Your misdirected rage,
The resultant head-hanging shame'n'guilt. A bit of new karma to be burnt.
The talking through it - for the moment, anyway. And an evening spent together:
Chinese takeout, videos from Kim's. And no more than a night of restless sleep.

The time of blue chicory flowers, G-d's current gift to the Jersey weedlots.
Hot humid days, evening downpours: the dog days, early. Your lectures beginning;
Still, you need to find a job. You will. For my part, I teach my own beliefs:
Acceptance. Trust. Floating downstream. Desire, too: a heart-connection.

If today's dark walls frighten, note changes, relax. You and I: we're not alone.

NYC - NJ
July 96

20.

(21) On Pride--I

There was a time, at fifteen, perhaps,
  When he read the good Dr. Reuben and was terrified, horrified,
  The emptiness, the loneliness, bowling alleys and public toilets,
  Silent loveless moments which - he was told - were all he could expect.

Later he read Ginsberg and was joyously turned on,
  "Kral Majales," "...Tuo Catullo," "Please Master,"
  Glorying in the poet's love-filled self, this true son of Whitman

(Auden's *"A Day for a Lay,"* found, appropriately, in '69:
  The gorgeous rhymes, perfectly-crafted stroke fantasy)

The reading brought him more poets with the same mad eyes for men,
  And reading the personals told him he wasn't alone.

In this video age, he sips hot red herbal teas, writes alone,
  Still reads the past, observes the ever changing, eternal present;
  The joys of sex/love, the poignancy of inevitable loss: our gay/human lives.

The sense, inextricably tied to the sex.
  The power of desire becoming strength of spirit,
  Mind opened by heart: the heaven of sweet total embrace.
  A healthy sexuality: an ever-healthier being.
  Body; Mind; Spirit; Love.

NYC
June - July 96

21.

(22) *Zipless*
for SFJ

It never happens anymore, not in this age of the plague,
But there it was, last night, midnight on First Avenue,
Me in my typically funky mood, worthless, detached - the East Village
Scene swirling around me, dully amused at the familiar void - and a bit of eye contact.

He walked across the street, noticed my almost-stare, noticed as I stopped,
Leaning lazily on a parking meter. I watched him almost-enter the bar,
Turn and cross, and, like a holy gift, walk directly back to me. A tattooed
Young Asian, crew-cut, very cute - and easily, back to my place.

No charades, no games, just fevered embrace: hot mutual desire.
His smooth hairless skin, his tight muscled body, his sweet hardness
Jutting out to be licked, to be swallowed. His tattooed arms, his
Nipple-ring; the pin in his scrotum! And hot. Horny. Just like me.

Trusting the requirements of safety, sheath-protected, his sword, almost-into my tightness.
Coming, by our own hands: the tongues; the touch. And it's over; he dresses, embraces, leaves.
Once the worst of our unattached lives, today so rare, incredibly sweet. Can't even
Dream of more. The random connection, pure trade of pleasure. A holy gift. For him. For me.

NYC
August 96

(23) Poem: for Vicki

It's as if I'd forgotten the first time
Voices of strangers riding our own hot rapids, our own hot endings
It's as if something deeper, stronger, seems to be newly forming
A seed of connection; a friendship, fueled by more than the promise of lust.

Secretive; the well-practiced fears. Of, *"the truth shall make them run."*
I do understand, though I'm opposite, freely shouting my madnesses,
Hoping those who care, will accept. Most do run; it's easy to let them go.
The gift: the risk of vulnerability, cradled in caring, supportive spirit.

Anticipatory as a lover, waiting the pleasures of our calls,
Enjoying the moving levels of talk, of trust, of desire.
Waiting that moment, the cool concrete garden, First Avenue,
Meeting you, as your twin. Recognizing the sweet, strong woman. Wanting you.

Dream of the meeting, of easy laughter, of mutual desire;
In my room, we kiss, deeply. We begin, as we began: tight: in each other's arms.

Rahway, NJ
September 96

(24) Preparing My Lover's Bed

for Andrea

Alone, her room,
She on the outside, doing her service,
Bob Marley, The Klezmatics, & Sophie B. as background
The household icons most definitely in control

The bed where we cuddled, last night, both tired,
(More like married than like hot new lovers),
Now preparing for her return, wanting her readiness,
Noting mine; awaiting her

Careful the folds, the white flowered sheet; smooth, not tight,
The woolen blanket, cream-woven flowers into warm brown earth,
The quilt of autumn, red and blue petals, serenely, on top
The quiet of the room; the quiet of the waiting

I don the warm thick robe, pad barefoot to shower;
Our space: prepared; ready. Waiting her return: the warmth of her bed.

Madison - Rahway, NJ
October 96

(25) *"Because Our Hearts Live In Our Bodies"*

We begin with what we're given, pale pigmented skin, deep red blood, genitalia seemingly important,
Karma gives us family & culture, shaping the clay of being into bones, eyes, desire,
Coming up through confusion, long breathing the dark foggy air of who-I-might-be,
I am who I am, tongue and heart, mind, body, soul; this work-in-progress, this poem yet unfinished.

History still living, faces & thighs of lovers no longer touched,
Anthony, Carol, with me only in poems & daydreams, remembered kisses & harsh, killing glares,
The past, the present, the precious warmth of a body pressing tightly on mine,
Pursuing, even now: the lovers who'll feed my body the healing touch it needs.

We live beyond these protein'd shells, on planes transparent to retina, to cortex,
Clear as melted tundra, as steam rising from hidden cave-springs, as salty tears from a child,
Vast reserves of limitless energy, the heart-stopping, life-wrenching orgasm a sigh compared!
We live those planes, but believe instead only this world. Our uniqueness: this human suffering.

The green light of heart be upon you, dear brothers and sisters:
To live the pains & pleasures of body, to equally seek higher. Our obligation: this human condition.

NYC - NJ
January 97

25.

Roz's Book:

In Celebration of

~~Fifty~~ <u>Sixty</u> Years

Second Edition

The title is, "Roz's Book."

So: who else should it be for?

DUH.

(31) Poem: for the Second Edition (Poem of the Book)

I really liked the original, even the concept, poems & photos, a clumsy black background,
But the poet in me thought this a way of getting the poems out to the people. I could teach myself:
I could learn to make these books. And I did; limited in scope, always costing more than they could
Possibly make; but I kept doing it, for me, for others; so we could have our words, out in the world.

Took the name from Ram Dass, after his stroke, *"It's all grace. But sometimes grace is very fierce."*
I once tried to sell these, finally gave up; now I ask strangers at trade shows or customer visits,
"May I give you a gift?" I wait: the odd looks, the cynical response, the walls going up: our culture.
I pass over the thin volumes, with the simple brown covers, smile: *"It's the computer in my bedroom."*

This book was the first for Fierce Grace; now there are fourteen titles, eight by me, six by others:
Pattie's haiku, Milby's dark bog-trampings, Alice's trust in a God who knows, and loves, beauty;
They have chapbooks, but never money from them; poets always need the day job, or a trust fund;
But what was only an odd gift for my sister, has now been revised: photos, illustrated by poems.

So much still the throwback, this digital age, putting out paper, not even a website to my name;
Yet there's that old-fashioned sweetness: holding a book in your hand. Reading; its own pleasure.

                                        Pooler, GA
                                        September 2010

(32) Author's Note (First Edition)

The original concept for this chapbook was a simple one--to put together some family photographs, illustrated by poems I'd written over the years, as part of a gift for my sister's 50th birthday. That being accomplished, I wanted the poems, at least, to see a wider audience--the photos were more personal, less universal. (Including the photos would've, of course, also made the publishing much more expensive.) The idea of putting the poems out in chapbook form, then, was with me even during the initial creation of the book; but life, as it will, and does, got in the way; just about a year passed before the single-copy gift book was transformed into this chapbook.

A little editing has taken place, akin to Ginsberg's *"...a method similar to manicuring grass that is removal of seeds and twigs, ands, buts, especially of's that don't contribute to getting the mind high;"* one poem was dropped from the original and three were added, giving a total of 21 (a lucky number) poems in this book. The oldest, a rather odd one from college, dates back to 1974; the book ends on a birthday poem from 1999. There are allusions to marriages, divorces, anniversaries, deaths, but mostly, like much of my writing, it's about continuing--*"just keep on keepin' on."* Some days, that's all we can do.

Some days, that's enough.

In love & light,

PL, Newark, NJ - Memphis, TN
August 2001

(33) *Invocation*

We begin. Becoming quiet.
One alone or creating the circle.
Consciously deepening breath, calming body, balance, being:
We begin. The safe space established. The opening of the door.

With sage and gladness, I call upon spirits of holiness, of joy,
Life givers, green and flesh, fire and heart,
Structure and more, light and spirit, generous, clear:
With sage and gladness, in welcome, in love. To join, in this, my home.

This door opens to the blessed, willingly sharing their kindnesses,
Entering silently, smiling, taking and giving openly, freely,
Barring all evil forces, repelling all depression and death;
This door denies all darkness. Negativity shall not blossom here.

This my home, my hearth, my spirit, my love;
This space allows truth, growth, service; the quiet, within. We have begun.

NYC
January - March 94

(34) (Untitled)

"My ancestors lived here for four generations."

"My ancestors were nameless, faceless Jews,
who lived small, quiet lives
shoemakers and tailors,
scientists and strikers

who were destroyed in the anger
who are preserved in the memory
in the memories of the lost ones
in the memories of the near-dead
in the nightmare of the terror
in the terrors of confusion
in the confusion of eternity

in the hellish torment of the fires and the caverns
in the life we see here, in this place, now."

"Oh, that's interesting," as he beat a hasty retreat

*   *   *   *   *

"Sure killed th' conversation, di'n'l?"

NYC
June 74

34.

(35) Grandparents, circa 1925

35.

(36) (Untitled)

Last night, on the sidewalks of heaven, my father the cabdriver picked up Jack Kerouac.
        Jack was drunk, of course, and my father didn't know who he was, of course,
        but Jack said, *"Take me to the Vieux Carre,"* and so, toward there,
        the yellow Heavenly Dodge drove

They drove over Michigan and South Carolina
Drove the highways of America
There's no time in heaven
There's no time in infinity
        (no time in eternity)

So, Jack got out, at the appointed time
Paid his cabfare / tipped handsomely
Looked for a convenient bar
Began reeling 'round N'Orleans

And the cabdriver
Who is my father
Turned the radio on to the Heavenly Jewish station
Turned his Heavenly Taxicab toward home
And arrived

        in his warm home
        with his shower
        his television set
        (his animal shows)
        his pleasures of life

All prepared
All waiting
Waiting only his arrival.

New Orleans
March 76

36.

(37) Parents & Grandparents, circa 1950

(37) Roz & Dad, circa 1952

(38) The Swimmer
for RLB, on her birthday

She's floating…
    Not at the beach, which is her home
    Though it can be good there:
        the hot summer days, the cool nights
        the black dog running easily, happily
        (a shadow almost seen: the young man)

She's floating…
    Not in the city, which is her work
    Though it can be difficult there:
        the word "professional" now gets a laugh
        "Are they all business calls?"
        (the back of a blue business suit: his abrupt exit)

She's floating…
    Not even in those memories, which is her past
    Though it can be painful there:
        the little apartments, the money fights
        the tough decision, finding her own truths
        (yellowing photographs: the young bride and groom)

She's floating…
    In her waking dreams, which is her future
    Though it must be unknown there
        the shadow adds definition, becomes a man
        a touch of the salesman, a bit more of the traveler
        (quite a lot of the comic: the one she will stay with)

They walk through the breaking surf
    for a moment they separate
        she's floating…
        he takes her hand
        slowly, calmly: they swim together.

NYC/October 84

(39) Woman on Beach

39.

(40) Real Wishes

for Roz & Tim

For each to grow in all ways, together and alone,
    and not to lose the other along the way

For each to lean on the other,
    for each to be supported by the other

For each to think of the other as himself,
    and each self as a part of the other

For both to remember your great love for the other,
    even in the midst of your angers

To free yourselves from financial worries,
    family burdens, emotional restraints

To find a bit of breathing space, to enjoy that special time,
    to learn of one another

To bring new life into the world, to watch it grow,
    become itself, with joy and pain

To live a long happy life,
    of quality, of serenity:

All these things, I do wish for you.

NYC
October 84

(41) The Duck Woman

I know now how it started, the classic transference,
From adored big brother to fuzzy blue duck

(Back then I couldn't imagine such feelings
Back then I couldn't own them of myself)

But images of ducks proliferated. Clocks, toys,
Paper towels. The Duck Woman took form.

We both ride the only river that truly matters,
Time, the Powerful. We each change and grow, within, without.

But our constant is the continuity of family;
Our strength comes from that closeness; our love from that same source.

NYC - NJ
June - July 87

41.

(42) Poem for Roz

"We know too well the woman;
We forget the child."

She is a woman, a struggling grown-up

    Her fights are of transit screw-ups, of payroll and political pressures, of
    Alternating moodiness, in herself and in her loves;
    Her year has given her blood at hand and foot, and
    The last exhalation of the poison gas

She is not alone. She feels so, sometimes.

She is a child, a hurting little girl

    Her dreams are yet to be realized, but
    Do breathe, brightly, within;
    Her days are solid, unspectacular, but
    Warm; loved; hopeful

She is not alone. She needs renewal, sometimes.

NYC
January 88

42.

(43) For Ken

"Y'ever get the feeling
We're just walkin' these paths,
Forgetting the glorious sunflowers, forgetting the cool spring skies,
Forgetting those many blessings we're all given,
Focusing only on the burdens we're forced to carry,
Tripping over stones and cursing our fate?"

"Sure. Sure, I feel that way, sometimes."

"Well—whad'ya do?"

"Whad'ya mean?"

"I mean—to get rid of it?"

"Oh. (Pause.) I talk about it. I give it time. (Pause.)
I hurt."

"Uh-huh. (Pause.) It passes, huh?"

"Usually does. For me."

"Uh-huh."

NJ
May 89

(44) Holiday Poem

To each of my friends, a wish:
> May each day bring you closer to yourself,
> Closer to the path which is real, and right, just for you,
>
> May you, and I, fill our lives with gentleness, and warmth,
> May we learn to give more, to smile more, to help;

We're all on the same road. May we learn to walk it together.

NYC
December 88

(45) Poem of Obsession / Poem of Hatred
for Bob

Even in late morning's gray light, the new purple blossoms, the hillside,
Even in the speeding ride, backed by Bird & C&W,
I hold on. I'm *"uncooperative."* I rage; impotent.

No understanding. Not even guessing why I'm here. Why I feel, thus.
Twisted images of power. Your rightness, my wrongness.
"Ultimate reality." Doubting. Continuing: fearfully. Blindly.

Worse than a jailer, a father, a G-d; inconstancy, disguised as helper.
Requiring more of me than me. Ever requiring more.
Progress? Perversity? Only terror, confusion, withdrawal.

I call out, to end the pain. It disappears, on letting go. I hold on.

Berkeley Heights, NJ
June 89

45.

(46) Poem of Positivity—II

for Debra

When I start to believe
When I no longer swallow the compassionate poisons
When I try the swirling currents, the too-deep waters
When I move beyond blasphemy, even approach surrender

Before the terrors overwhelm me
I will understand

When you struggle with your everyday
When you taste the black bitterness of the brave new rapids
When you burn with the sudden sharp steel of your own will
When you move beyond complacency, even approach acceptance

Before the familiar immobilizes you
You will rise above

When we live humbly with ourselves
When we learn the tiny miracles that the ordinary can offer
When we trust quietly in the power of the unseen benevolence
When we move beyond the mire, even approach our new freedom

Before the gift of this time is lost
We will know the radiance

NYC - NJ
July - September 89

46.

(47) On Creation: A Re-Telling

Darkness, Darkness: an eternity of darkness.

Before there was light, before there was art, before there was image, before there even was the Word:
there was the Sound. The Sound contained all the sounds that would ever be heard for all time

In a billionth of a picosecond, all was heard:
Elvis Presley, Jerry Lee Lewis, Guy Lombardo,
A young cricket, a dying lion, a slaughtered sheep,
The ocean, the Concorde, a child's laughter at the park,
The dealmaking words of an agent, Crosby's crooning,
The moans of lovemaking, a crone's cackle,
Sounds of pain, joy, frustration, bitter sorrow,
I love you and wop-bobba-loo-bop,
Your Cheating Heart and My Troubled Mind,
Drinking Again and John Barleycorn Must Die,
The prayers of millions of lips, from the million desperate tongues

The sound was jubilant and joyful, arrogant, humble, and all-inclusive. The sound grew from that
spot where it began *(may no man ever know that place!)*, moved outward at speeds beyond
conception, carrying planets, moons, mountains, oceans: the primordial soup, that necessary
organic broth, existed on millions of planets, carbon DNA here, arsenic RNA there, billions and
billions of lives in this universe, some living the sounds, some worshipping the silence:

All we know
All we ever can be
Is the sound

The sound
The Sound of the Universe
The Sound: the unpronounceable Sound.

Rowe Camp, MA
November 89

47.

(48) "Challenges"
for Arlene

To face each new day, secure in its new promise
To dance freely, painlessly, teaching the body new limits
To buy the land, create the space, to build the home of your own
To always, always rise. To **shine:** your own power and glory.

To bring your ever-new self to the city's dull asphalt
To sing your essential living truth, the potential of diversity
To co-create new life, open to strength, health, and love
To grow in that same love, to breathe within that spirit:

To continue: this life; your life: today.

Berkeley Heights, NJ
November 90

48.

(49) For Ilene

Child of the moon,
Susceptible to the tides, to strangely dark, inexplicable pulls,
To pressurings; into tears. Into crushing, unlovable, dark hurts.

But rarely, only. More, you're the dependable,
The giver of valiant effort, the too-many hours;
The giver of your heart. Always, the giver of your heart.

Summer new again, the sweaty, crowded Port, your always-busy home;
And again, my sister, I offer my heart. Always, I offer my heart.

Rahway NJ
July 95

(50) Poem: for Nazareth

To live this small, quiet life
     As though every breath, every movement
     Solitary, or especially among others
     Consciously chosen, to be of maximum service:
The Holy Will of G-d

Being human, can't fully know that Will for me
Being human, must live fully, all the limited needs

To live this small, quiet life
     As though health and giving truly matter
     Never knowing if this odd rockiness truly serves
     But trusting. Believing. Invisible direction, support:
Failure's inevitable

Lightly, love-filled, accepting this path
Lightly, love-filled, moving forward: the rockiness as joy.

Convent Station, NJ - NYC
May - August 94

(51) PL with Big Buddha, Kent, NY

(52) For Roz & Tim: Ten Years

Marriage a contract, a commitment, a well-charged gift:
      each to the other

Time, the testing ground, a rocky path, the proof:
      the sacred fire

Together the constant creation, the yearnings, the growings alone:
      the hardest: the growings, as one

Marriage / time / together:
      beyond pains or joys: the loving spirit: the living heart.

NYC
November - December 94

(53) The Three-Thousand Mile Garden
for Ryn

The current morning ritual: coffee, check e-mail,
Often, joyfully, finding your reply

We've done this for a while, we're continuing;
Connecting. Laughter, histories, occasional complaints

The pink-and-white spring flowers: the East
The ever-present redwoods, the eternal sea: the West

You, and I: our private, living garden.

Convent Station, NJ
May 2006

(54) (Untitled)

We all want it
Want it fast, want it easy

Want it to pay the rent
Want it for the books and the CD's
Want it for the tuition and for the VISA bills
Want it for the color tv, the VCR, the CD player, the microwave
Want it for the dinners, the movies, the cappucinos, the hookers
Want it all. Now.
Want it all. Now.

Gotta go job to get it
Gotta go job, damn subway or traffic commute
Gotta go job, dull & boring or hot & stressful
Gotta go job, selling & buying, drug dealing or word processing
The money that we need. For our many, many wants.
The money that we need. For our many, many wants.

It's never easy. And it always goes so fast.
Doesn't stop us from wanting it

NYC
February 96

54.

(55) A Bus Named Desire, New Orleans

(56) Moving On: A Poem of Rockaway
for Langston Hughes

Once I thought I was of the ocean

Standing alone at water's edge, the comforting thunder,
    the gray-green god sighing to my feet,
    knowing all my heart's truths echoed in his silent, gray-green depths;
    dreaming that singular freedom:
    living the two-legged life with the heart of the sea

Today I think I'm of the shore

At my best at that interface, mud and spirit,
    the solitary pilgrimage over winter sands,
    this personal Sinai leading to this personal holy land;
    but today the gray-green god is separate, a glorious thing outside;
    always a master; no longer mine

What I will think doesn't matter, earth or ocean, less or more
Comfort comes from choosing our beliefs; power from believing our choices.

NYC
April - June 96

56.

(57) Rockaway Beach Triptych

(58) Pacific Coast Highway

(59) "Personal Peace"
as suggested by LB

It's the subliminal need for water, I'm sure,
Maybe the tides, the moon, the impeccably balanced spin, keeping me safe, this blue planet's surface;
I come again, the familiar spit of sand, the brackish bay, the airport across;
In the distance--Emerald City. Glorious excess, lights, colors--the dream, still living--New York City.

To physically place myself , this place of safety, security, serenity,
A place not of confrontation nor resolution, but simply of being: open, clear, accepting,
The gift of calm quietness, the low hum of the planes, the water slapping at the pier,
Pre-verbal, not thought, knowledge, understanding; the well-practiced calmness, of simply: *here.*

Or the shore, the crashing ocean, or alone in my car, the speeding blacktop below my wheels,
The same effortless ease-of-being clearly, *"as it's s'posed to be."*
Seemingly accessed by external place, it's internal mind which gives this centering, this comfort,
And the light of gentle Spirit, beyond place or mind, remains the ultimate, life-giving source.

Watch the drama of the shifting of moods, laughter, death, Visa bills and sweet, sweet loving:
All real, all valid; all limited. The joy-filled, solemn, centering silence: available to all.

Nyack - Croton, NY
March 99

59.

(60) "Y'Say It's Your Birthday"
for Roz

This year it follows the New Year, two aspects of a new beginning,
But rather, you're in the midst of a somewhat uncomfortable limbo.
For today, the path must be a somewhat comfortable continuance,
But the inevitable approaches. And Major Change waits, quietly, for you.

Major Change. And this year brought you Elvis and Sweet Pea,
The loss of the landlord, foot surgery and asthma.
Another year of deep abiding love, with the anger & silences of marriage,
But Tim's sweet goodness, even in the midst of growth: comforts. Strengthens. Supports.

And Major Change; waiting. To stand at the edge of the ocean, trusting in the process,
To know you're a part of this infinite thread, a breathing light connected to the All.
Just another being; just another day. But awareness: the amazing brightness, the ordinary,
Another birthday. And middle age approaches. You, somewhere in the middle of your life.

This year'll be low on material gifts, funds're low all around;
But love & honor, respect & trust: these I offer you, this special, this ordinary day.

Ossining - Hawthorne, NY
September 99

60.

(61) For the Invisible Jew
for Larry

When I saw you in the hallway, I saw your father's face
Told you that later, in Alice's apartment; you said Paul had said the same
78: how long can a man live? Sick at the end, which is common; we all pass,
Gone, now, and gone too—the last of that generation. Your parents. Mine. Now Alice's, too.

Last time I'd seen you must've been her wedding. I'd grumbled in New York, not wanting
      to go down, but I did, my wide body still living in fading color photos.
You were there, but we barely spoke. Cousins, never close enough to be friends,
The difference of four years mattered strongly as kids, not at all now;
Now, again self-described: a religious Jew. Your white hair, thin; our histories burn, in the
      old photos. Today, my salt & pepper beard gives the lie: the deep black, of 1981.

So, we both now agree strongly to walk the walk, to stay in touch; we've heard this before,
But now this seems real. I don't know you now, I know your face as your father's face but
      have no clue as to who you are, today,
Who you'd loved and what you'd smoked and where you'd lived and what you'd dreamed and
      all of the stuff that makes up your history, makes you who you are, today;
And you're just as blind to all the stuff that makes me, today.

You're a middle-aged white-haired Jew, just as I am. You're my family, just as I'm yours.
Dysfunctional, of course. And only a few of this family left.
So we begin: here. As Paul rests in the ground next to Sylvia,
As together, we help choose a name for baby Ryan.

Welcome back to this small, aging family.
Welcome back from the land of apartness.

Charlotte, NC – White Plains, NY
December 2006

(62) Pooler, Saturday Afternoon

Heavy black clouds dominate the sky, clearly alive, sentient
Obvious that these powerful, conscious beings control the sky, the day;
Of course it'll rain. But it won't rain until the clouds choose to do so;
Years ago, on 12th St., I stood watching, writing, just as now--waiting for the rain.

New York music from my computer--Jonathan Schwartz, that comforting, cultured presence,
Satchmo asking a kiss to build a dream on; Eckstein taking a chance on love;
It's the American Songbook, alive and well, technology serving us here nobly, spirit still strong,
Tuesday I'll see Bucky, Alden, and Peplowski--the Usual Suspects--at the Savannah Music Fest.

The wind picks up noticeably, with a giveaway chill. And here's the rain,
Onto the sidewalk, the lake, coldly, into my screened-in porch.
Steve Post now playing some old nasty blues, offering a remembrance of the great Theodore,
The wind rising, giving the lake a tidal illusion; the air now a thick, dark gray. The southern shower.

The ancients had it right, I think--respect the power, these elemental forces: floods in Fargo,
Volcanoes, earthquakes, tornadoes; at the whims of the masters. Tiny humans--just trying to hold on.

Pooler, GA
March 2009

62.

(63) Eighty
for David

Rockaway's the right place for you, nine stories above, overlooking the great and wondrous ocean:
Always been part of you. Lifeguarding, a thousand years ago. The plate reading *"Swimer."*
Sailors, landlubbers both know, while its face appears to change, darken, crest, calm,
What it is, never changes. It contains us, includes us; as close to eternity as any we'll know.

It's one a'those seemingly significant birthdays: an "0" at the end. But the day's no more meaningful
Than yesterday, or the almost 30K days already lived. You spent many early days in carousing & riot,
And stopping drink didn't change the fear, the terrified fetal crouch; seemingly alone, nowhere to go;
'Cause jumping off the roof would've hurt, you came into the rooms, stayed; now you live by the book.

"You and I, we'll never retire, we'll work to the end," you told me once, recall it often, believe it,
Both for you, and for me. I watch you show the way ahead. You've got a twenty-year head start,
I keep watching you, respecting those who came before: Bechet. Pops. Dexter & Stan. Bob & Bill.
What mattered, still matters. Nikki. The hearings, tomorrow. The 37 pharmaceuticals; just for today.

If I'd ask you, I'd guess you'd say, you still don't know what it's all about;
I believe you, yet both you and I keep working, keep showing up, keep doing the next right thing:

Have a Very Happy Ordinary Day.

Savannah - Pooler, GA
July 2010

(64) Saxophone, Sixth Avenue, NYC, circa 90

(65) I've Listened...
for Larry

Long ago, maybe the early 80's,
I smoked while visiting with a polar bear, Central Park Zoo
Buzzed, I walked down to Carnegie as the light snow fell gently,
Heard Sonny Rollins leading his young strong band: *"a proud man, playing a big horn"*

A couple of years earlier, a stadium in Tucson,
I'd dropped something-or-another before a Fleetwood Mac concert,
Watched the tall amp-stands turn into H. R. Pufnstuf monsters,
But they were friendly, harmless; they actually added some background guitar & bass

With Larry, after a long night of drinking, NYC,
We wandered into Illinois Jacquet's near-deserted club, 58th Street,
Caught the end of the set, the boss' big band, mostly young guys, knew their books well;
The sound was great, but musicians ain't businessmen; the empty club closed soon after

In Savannah, I've seen Bob Seeley, the 80-year old boogie-woogie master, *"a force of nature,"*
Saw Kenny Barron, solo piano, at the Festival; his elegant, well-controlled artistry,
Heard a little sweet samba at the Westin across the river, tasteful, quiet, piano, drums & vocal,
I guess I really didn't need all that stuff in me--the music, after all, will out.

And in the warm little apartment, Pooler, there's vinyl, tapes, CD's, Jonathan Schwartz on computer;
Perhaps the greatest gift of the many that've been given; spent a lifetime listening...I'm still listening.

Pooler, GA
February 2010

65.

(66) Wedding Poem
for Bob & Debbie

"Dance me: to the end of love"
Leonard Cohen

Everyone has their cauldron filled with histories; none of them matter, today
Everyone has their thundercloud of futures; these also, matter not, this day
Today is the day of our power, today is the moment, our action; today, before this assembled group,
The change begins, the ritual giving the framework-- the man, the woman, giving it life.

There's no doubt that they'll know warm Caribbean vistas, frozen ice-white ski-trails,
Rocky gravel roads, hairpin twists over dark ancient mountains; too, they'll know ordinary days,
Days of bill-paying and laundry, of car repairs and veterinarians. But something new shall be added,
            after this day:
The ordinary and the mysterious, the noise of this world and the quiet of others; all now to be lived,
            as two-become-one.

And the bride and groom will dance the first dance as one, and this love, born years before,
            shall grow, shall shine,
And these two, forever individual, will also become one. The mystery of this sacrament;
             this power created by love
The good wishes of all assembled here: energy becoming energy, strengthening, supporting,
            these two, this one;
Our love will remain with them as flakes of silver, as the foam of the ocean; as the happy laughter
            of a tiny bird.

Repetition creates tradition, traditions grow into ritual; ritual may serve the many generations:
To use the good of old creation, to make it into the new, to build lives of health and strength,
            compassion and love:

Trust your bodies. Trust your minds. Trust your spirits.
The power, the glory, the sweetness; your amazing, limitless, two-centered love.

Savannah, GA – East Brunswick, NJ
September – October 2008

(67) "You Don't Look Your Age"
for Roz, at 60

You don't act it, either; know you don't feel it, and when I call you, *"old"* I'm right there behind you,
Anyway, when I say that it's only as a semi-joking pejorative, true for both of us: like, *"short."*
But there's some truth there; we both remember the day Kennedy was shot, and our co-workers,
Born in '85, have no clue of our times, of the concerts we saw; of the presidents we remember.

So, while we both know that *"age ain't nothin' but a number,"*
Much of today's culture evades us; neither you nor I neither text (much) or tweet.
Your life was shaped in the 50's and 60's, in Brooklyn and at Far Rock High,
And while you were too straight to be a hippie, I still remember--it was you who first turned me on.

The ongoing reality is that health is always an issue; you've taken a big step this year,
Lots of weight lost--not the easiest process, but you're working it, you keep doing it.
So the life you lead today seems still a matter of just going to the job, of dinners with Tim & friends,
Maybe AC with the chil-der-en; there's nothing wrong with playing games--and having a good time.

There's a quote on my wall, *"Other things may change us, but we start and we end with family;"*
The words and photos give a taste, our history, but the totality of our lives remains within ourselves;
Fortunate that we three've chosen to remain close; mind, heart, spirit. Disagreements do arise--
36 hours can be a very long time--but we remain family. And the family remains.

Pooler, GA
September 2010

THE HOLIDAY POEMS

1986 - 2005

With additional poems 2007 - 2018

For all of my family;
For all of my friends;
For all those I've remembered;
For all those I've forgotten;

All we have is today.
Let's celebrate today.

Author's Note (Second Edition)

I'd never done a second edition of any of my books before, but for years I've kept printing them and giving them away. (I've mostly given up on the idea of selling them; as had been said, *"for someone to be a poet in America today, he/she needs one of two things: a day job or a trust fund.*) I often surprise near-strangers--people whom I've barely met--with the rather odd question, "*May I give you a gift?"* The answer is usually yes, if a rather confused yes; and that's when I pull a chapbook or two out of my bag. It's one way of getting the poem on the printed page out into the world.

During the last five years, I've found that I'd written fewer poems than I had in the past, questioning more and more why it is that I write in the first place. But these are "Holiday Poems," though, and it's easier to answer that question in this specific case: I write to connect, to tell friends and family and semi-strangers that I'm still here, that I've still got something to say, and that I still care, as we've trudged or skipped or danced or struggled through another year. As a teacher of mine reminds us, *"life is supposed to be fun!"* Use this book for pleasure. Enjoy these poems. And further, enjoy the choices that you've made. and the choices you continue to make. And if they were wrong, correct them, with joy & laughter & forgiveness, and just move on. As Paul Simon has said, *"have a good time."*

Philadelphia - Ft. Lauderdale, FL
December 06

Author's Note (First Edition)

Well, it's Christmas. Or, if you're PC: "the Holiday season." (PC is such nonsense, though.) I'm not a Christian—I was born into JC's original tribe, so that's part of who/what I am—but it is a cultural celebration. Christmastime. Lights. Snow. Times Square, the ball dropping. Dick Clark, with that mysterious portrait hidden in a closet somewhere. Resolutions (yes, this is the year I'll lose the weight—*right*). And cards. Always the cards.

Some friends complain about the cards, as a part of the commercialism of Christmas, but I've always liked that part. In the past two or three years, I've gotten more folks sending me a separate sheet with an update on their lives; I find this useful because I have many friends/acquaintances that I don't see for years & years—it's a way of staying in touch. The poems in this book were written/sent over the last 16 years. They're not great poems, perhaps—they're the stuff you'll find in a card to a friend—but I like to think that there's growth. I think I'm writing better in 2002 than I was in 1986. I hope so, anyway.

There are other holidays. The Jewish New Year. Chanukah. Solstice. Equinox. Each of these was, at least once or twice, a reason to write a poem. There were times (1987, '89, '94, '99, and 2001) in which I sent friends a cassette tape along with my card—just passing on some music that worked for me. They tended to be heavy on Bob Dylan, Paul Simon, Billy Joel, maybe a little Dizzy Gillespie; maybe one Xmas song just to justify its existence as a "Christmas tape." Sometimes the poem was written *as* backup for the music *("For the Holidays, With Music: 1994,"* as an example); sometimes they were independent of each other; they just happened to be in the same envelope. This year, the plan was not to send a tape, but rather, this book. The tapes worked as little stocking-stuffers, sometimes— maybe this'll work in the same way.

I'm writing this on Labor Day Weekend, 2002. It's been a hot summer; the one-year anniversary of 9/11 is less than two weeks away. It'll be Christmastime when you read this; enjoy the holidays, but know: all in time passes. It's only today—it's only this moment. Enjoy this moment. Make it better, for yourself, & for those around you. Live peace. Live love.

Croton-on-Hudson, NY
September 2002

(75) Poem for Oakite: Christmas

for all of us

I'm tired of year-end clichés, of company goals met
    and the much that remains to be done

And though the sky is a cloudless blue mirror, the air is chill,
    stark gray branches cry the season and the feeder should be filled

These are vacation days, of home, and family, and reflection,
    of past; of future; of quietly accepting the now

The clichés are of endings and beginnings
    of the inexorable timeclocks which do support us

It must be Christmas. We begin, again.

Berkeley Heights, NJ
December 86

75.

(76) End of Year Poem

for the people of Oakite

It doesn't yet feel like Christmas.

Yet it does feel like December, with its chilly rains,
        Sunday football, and the hollow silences of dying cars

But within the bright labs, the turnings of the seasons mean little.
        In the service of the centers of profit, we struggle, as one;
        we do create the new. We hope that they'll sell.

And the work rises before us, work of balancing the powers of material,
        work of steering the subtly shifting waters;

We aim for progress, growth,
        for some measure of success;

The days of the year come to an end. The task continues.

NYC - Berkeley Heights, NJ
December 87

(77) Poem: for the Holidays

The chill of new autumn; the holidays, again.
To take the time, to look at ourselves,

To admit our wrongs. To hope for real change.
We pray for right living, pray to be inscribed:

Alone, and together; G-d and His people;
We do the ritual. Somehow, it does still matter.

NYC
September 89

(78) Holiday Poem (with Additional Music)

We are given choices.

There must be evil; it must be faced;
       Yet it may be assuaged, by the holy waters.

In the City, he learns behavior:
       Teased by the fruits of work, and love.

That most gentle angel offers all, yet only
       "Willingness is the key" to her special light.

Arriving again at the season, he still believes;
       Laughter, hope, trust in our Selves;

"We shall be happy."

NYC - NJ
December 89

(79) For the Holidays: 1990

"To savor
Our personal light
Through dark snowfall, through warming sun

To trust
Our chosen direction
Through ocean's anger, through vision's pain

To love
The best part of ourselves
Through breakups and bring-downs, through silliness and sense;

Through the gift of every living moment of our days."

NYC - Berkeley Heights, NJ
December 90

(80) Coffee Shop Poem
for Charlene

Feeling slightly guilty

French toast and beef sausage in the empty coffee shop of my dream
    Johnny Mathis: *"Wonderful, Wonderful"* on CBS oldies

Watching staff exchange gifts
    Guessing at their warmth; their closeness

Smiling; eavesdropping;
    The watcher at his quiet booth

Others enter: eggs over medium; fries: *"C'n I get a tea wit' dat—"*
    Back to the necessary work

Real, as Christmas. Real, as moving on.

Newark, NJ
December 91

80.

(81) Holiday Poem: 1991

In this time of remembering miracles:
        Lights out of nothingness
        G-d becoming infant

Quietly living our own tiny miracles:
        Laughter on hard city streets
        Intimacy available, in openness, in love

Our lives: the constant uphill struggle of desire
        The miracle lies beyond mere survival
        The miracle is embracing the joy.

NYC - NJ
December 91

(82) Poem: for the New Year (1993)

As precious, recurring gift of the season,

    We find ourselves here, again
    The threshold of creation's birthday,
    The inter-loving fabric of our many diverse lives:

Wishing sweetness, health, remembrance: daily, lifelove.

                      NYC
                      September 93

(83) Poem for the Holidays: 1993

*"We are holy beings
surrounded by holy beings."
—Stan Dale*

The living bottom of the ocean, cold winter morning
The technological heart of a silver airship, mid-flight
The subtle chemical vibrations connecting man and woman

She (He) wants so much, stability, love, accomplishment
He (She) carries this burden, dysfunction and damage
Their meeting can only be in the warm room of love

Our culture's creative, wide ranging, but
Our real lives, our hearts, barely touched; and yet:
Our path to the light shall re-create, shall empower us all.

Boston - NYC - Kearny, NJ
December 93

83.

(84) Poem: for the New Year (1994)

Early this year, this quieting time,
Time away from deadening work,
Time to praise, to remember, the living, the dead;

The family together, spirit if not flesh;
The circle ends, begins anew.

The celebration: Rosh Hashonah. Again.

NYC
September 94

(85) Equinox
for Chris and Wendy

On this night when even our spinning home is silently, perfectly balanced
We salute the quarters, the holiness and nobility therein:

    The East, Mecca, Jerusalem, the gentle holy bo tree
    The West, the Great Plains, peyote, the blue cavernous Pacific
    The North, New England colors, permafrost, Jack's grave in Lowell
    The South, the *Vieux Carre*, Rio, the dynamic coral-life – the dark Caribbean

Choosing to visit here, this place, this time,
The synergy of our spirits, creation: this original, newly-formed Unity:

    Laughter, warm music: autumn again, rejoicing, New York City
    The play beyond thought; shadows, smiles, connecting strangers
    Opening hearts, vulnerabilities; intimacies of new friendship and trust
    Each a discrete presence, each a single breathing cell; this greater spiral

On this night of balance, the gift is the mystery, the glory; these ordinary things:
Our bodies, our beings, only seem separate; in truth, none of us shall ever be alone.

                                                     NYC
                                                     September 94

(86) Chanukah Poem

Remembering the miracles
Somehow it still matters: to know I'm a Jew

Past land or politics; past sad comic stereotypes
What matters lives in family; in memory; in the many long past

At festivals, we sing His praises
Our glorious, silent G-d

What does this mean, today: to know that I'm a Jew?
The candles give their light. We trust in their light—we trust in our truth.

NYC
November 94

\

(87) For the Holidays, with Music: 1994

To be out of love, Christmastime:
    a special melancholy: a slave to memory

But limbo gives way, the necessary change:
    emotional road trip: for pleasure, alone!

Beyond our culture's goodness, beyond its barren heart,
    living breath, true light: shining sweetly, healthy; real

Politically incorrect, this vision, but mine, strongly mine:
    joy, 'midst illusion: the ongoing connection. My many noble friends.

NYC
December 94

(88) Poem for the New Year (1995)

Trust in the setting of the orange sun,

    Trust the loving shore, the moving ocean;

Know that G-d lives. Trust always, in Him.

NYC
September - October 95

(89) Holiday: 1995

These are busy times for me; for you,
as well. Work and money and self-
improvement and meetings and phone
calls and movies and concerts and
dinners and coffee and talking and
listening and hot herbal baths and
meditation and prayer and laundry and
television and writing poetry and work
and money and car and VISA bills and
weekends of love in New England; busy
times, indeed. And I don't make the time
to write, to call, to talk, to tell you what
I'm going through, to listen to you, my
dear, dear friend, to what you're going
through, to be there for you and with you,
to make the real connections, to brightly live
that special commitment which is our
friendship; but the gift remains the
continuance, its diversity, its imperfections;
the gift is the circle, which is our earth,
which is the year, which is
where we are, again:

**Health. Warmth. Peace.
Chanukah. Christmas. Solstice.
Today.**

NYC - NJ
December 95

89.

(90) Holiday Poem: 1996

The road:
      Following black asphalt, the painted white line
      The star-filled blackness becoming shining mid-day

      The passing of miles, green hills, night-dark sea,
      Trusting only in movement, in growth, & change; in life & love;

      Believing in pain & struggle as necessary lessons, no less the gift
      Than the lover's kiss, the honest laugh, the happy, tired sigh;
The holidays.

Still on the road; still moving forward.

NYC - NJ
December 96

90.

(91) Solstice
for Wendy and Chris

"Everything dies, baby that's a fact
but maybe everything that dies
someday comes back."
—Springsteen, "Atlantic City"

We forget so much. We believe in internal combustion and silicon wafers, in their
    power & their teachings, in the comforts & knowledge they bring us. But we
    forget the old ones; the visions on the hellish deserts of the Great Plains,
    the rites of becoming by the Congo River, the stars, our Sun:
    Stonehenge. Mexico City. Alexandria.

There's much that is good here. Our culture is strong & diverse, we glory in our material solace,
    our homes and meeting-rooms are clean, well-kept, safe from fire and winds,
    our foods are satisfying & supportive, our telescreens show us all parts
    of our shrinking global village—but we're starving in this palace of plenty.
    We're empty in this world of fulfillment.

It's not needed that we turn our backs on this, our living time—this, the world we've
    been given. To walk away from a gift offends the Giver, and damages each of
    us, more. But to value the movement of the holy Sun, to honor it and join
    with others, in remembrance, in communion, to share, and re-create;
    the old ways yet useful, in this, our living time;

Embracing spirit in the midst of technology: the millennium, rising.

NYC - Rahway. NJ
June 97

91.

(92) Holiday Poem: 1997

We think memory's just a video:
        The times I knew love
        The living beach, hot humid August
        The smiles of proud parents, now thirty years gone

But science now knows: experience feeds our souls, our cells:
        Evil words become vicious, ass-biting gremlins
        Old satisfactions yield serenity, light, lowered blood pressure
        That kiss freely given, 1974: feel the warmth, the heart-opening, 1997

We change, we move, we grow: that's normal
But know: our changes continue to live, silently: re-creating us

Past and future living always, always, the eternal Now;
The calendar's limited reality. A time to remember. In love.

Chanukah. Christmas. Solstice.
Today.

Morrisville, PA
December 97

92.

(93) Holiday Poem: 1998

"The end is nothing.
The road is all."
--Nelson Algren – epitaph

It's a limited sight distance, this bend I'm on;
But rolling. Leaves now gone, bare silent trees at highway-side,
Oddly warm for December; living powerful, ongoing constancy-of-change,
Unconcerned about ends. Rolling. Forward? Not sure. Maybe. Hopefully.

Beachfront, winter. Alone, just me & the damned seagulls,
The speeding sandpipers, the seaweed-covered, slick jetty-rocks;
The eternal ocean. Trust: its liquid solidity, its constancy-in-change,
A vision, a tool, a centering: beyond road's many bends. My true living home.

Rising past fear's ugly grin, risking more, to grow, to give:
Again, the turning of the year. Another step, this my own, my given road.

Chanukah. Christmas. Solstice.
Today.

Westchester County, NY
December 98

(94) Holiday Poem: 1999

"The stars are matter
We're matter
But it doesn't matter."
—Capt. Beefheart

Maybe he's right; maybe all of it, maybe it doesn't matter,
Even though it all seems to matter so much, so many levels, so much to do (so it seems);
"Shut your mouth & listen." Excellent advice. Quiet the mind, learn to be still;
Learning to float downstream, to take right action. Developing discernment.

Millennium. Neither ending, nor beginning; continuation.
Technology's speed & power remains, the driving force of this semi-mad culture,
But what really matters is individual growth, the collective human spirit,
        the single unified breathing soul,
Gentleness: as beings; as species. Positive action, daily. Each living being a creator of change:

"...in the midst of pain, we have learned the importance of laughter."
Ram Dass' teaching, in me; for you. The gift is today; the gift is you.

Chanukah. Christmas. Solstice.
New Year. K'wanzaa.
Today.

Croton-on-Hudson, NY
November 99

94.

(95) Holiday Poem: 2000

"I'm glad to be here.
I'm glad to be anywhere."
—John Gulick

The old car rolls up to Charles Point, again,
China Pier, the river, the lights of the bridge over to Rockland,
Chill the December air, the living water; this holy place, this temple;
This practice: revisiting, the centering place. Continuing: this ongoing, internal work.

The well-practiced checklist, how'm I doin'?: work, love, money, play, service: people;
Emptying. Allowing the silence, the stars, the cold moist river-air, to fill, to re-create me;
This stuff I busy my life with, all the many desires, the fears, the tiring, sad, daily struggle;
For meaning; for reason; for usefulness; for happiness. For this moment: this here; this now.

December, again. Y2K long gone, our speedy, power-charged culture burning; alone,
Somewhere: on the surface of our planet. Somewhere, in the midst of our lives. Refreshed, again;
Leaving this personal, open-air temple; back to the old car, the one-bedroom, the job, tomorrow;
A prayer for loving-kindness, for all life, this tiny blue planet. Communication. Connection.

Chanukah. Christmas. Solstice. K'wanzaa.
Today.

Westchester County, NY
November - December 2000

95.

(96) Out of the Ashes

"We need to fight
But more: we need to love."
—PL, July 00

All the teachers who know, say:
Everything passes. Don't hold on. Learn letting go, learn to flow;
An' I believe 'em, I do: just so hard: that simplicity; that ease-of-being

'Cause while I'm here: always, it's the search. It's the here & now, yeah, but
It's also, always, the search. Work. Love. What to do, now; where to go, next? Why?

And though the heart is open, and ready for love, there's anger,
Hatred. Greed. Fear. Co-existing: these generous days; these unquiet nights.

The way out, they say, is only the way through;
Living each day as if it were your last, or even your first; imperfect lives; imperfect world.

It's snowing. Snowing. Summer's long gone; it'll come again, but now:
Winter, again. The Holidays. With changes: in climate. In culture. In character.
We remember.   We hold each other, touch each other, with words, with heart, with spirit:

That which is good, shall continue to grow.
Christmas. Chanukah. Solstice. K'wanzaa.
Today.

Westchester County, NY
November 2001

96.

(97) Poem for the Holidays: 2001

In the midst of all the uncertainty   In the midst of all the activity
Our gloriously complex lives   These interesting days
Airplanes falling from the skies
Fires in Rockaway, fires at Ground Zero
CNN, the day job, and a grande chai at Barnes & Noble

In the midst of all the speed   In the midst of all the noise
Need: against the grain   Need: to seek the quiet
Need to pull back from the marketplace
To close your eyes. Re-charge. Re-commit:
Alone: center: the many blessings; this culture; our lives

In the midst of all the loneliness   In the midst of all the family
Questioning going forward   We will go forward
Beyond all of the suffering, beyond all of the gifts
This life a sorrow-filled banquet, a potential, an instant:
All that we ever need, or want: available, always: right here; right now:

Chanukah. Christmas. K'wanzaa. Solstice.
Today.

NJ - NY
November 2001

97.

(98) Holiday Poem: 2002

for Rocco & for Charlie

"And, in the end: the love you take
is equal to the love you make."
—Lennon/McCartney

It's been a busy year, workin', travelin',
Florida twice, LA twice, Vermont, Chicago, Maine and NOLA;
Continuing, trying: righting old wrongs; remaining in the moment;
Never needed glasses before—reluctant acceptance: middle age.

My small life today's about learning & teaching: our products, our colors;
Of contributing, our community: poets, painters, musicians, artists;
Of giving, the small ways: coffee, chairs, window shades, the steps;
The difficult dance of would-be lovers. Trusting; learning: letting go.

Work & love & fun & loss; grateful: for friends past, for those not yet met;
This busy, active, willing time. So much left to do; we'll do what we can.

Croton-on-Hudson, NY
November 2002

(99) The Last Day of the Year

It's a Tuesday, but the company calls it a holiday
    sleep in, play, read

Zukav's **Soul Stories**, slowly, savoring;
    music. Going through old vinyl,

Joan Baez's amazing voice;
    Paquito, tenor & bass only, *"God Rest Ye…"*

Breakfast. I'll shower, shave, later
    will go out, do the errands

Keys to be made, oil change, laundry
    1:30, roads damp, still some fog

Christmas cards: leave a dozen or so on display;
    others arranged gently: a flat square pile

Time: to take the time. The year, again,
    "Goals: 2002" on my wall

Reducing the year to numbers, accomplishments
    To tasks ~60% completed

No. A year of long, complicated, intricate days
    I've made mistakes, had some successes,

I've touched some. Angered some.
    Shared deep, healthy, loving hugs with a few

It's end of year, the accountants close the books:
    we, who still can, continue

There is hope, and health, and strength;
    the mystery of tomorrow. We will continue.

The First Day of the Year

And I awoke easily, mid-morning
    this brand new day/month/year

Last night spent quietly, coffee &
    conversation, the diner, early

Then alone, the snow-covered pier
    the river; for centering; for quiet

And home, tv, bouncing from "Insomniac"
    to "Twilight Zone" to "History of Sex"

Switched to Leno a minute before, saw
    the countdown, ball drop, the confetti

Images of red-white-and blue,
    not the usual drunken revelry

And sleep, early. And waking, the book; again,
    new concepts for me to practice:

Intention. For harmony, cooperation,
    sharing, reverence for Life;

Taking it in, slowly. Thinking:
    this book may be as important as

Be Here Now. Soul Prints.
    Books which've truly changed me

Cold rain, gray fog, river almost hidden;
    A quiet day. Reading. Writing. Music.

And the intention: to create the better world.
    The way: a better me, Only: for today .

Croton-on-Hudson, NY/December 2002 - January 2003

(100) Holiday Poem: 2003

in remembrance of Pepper

*"I don't have everything I want,
but I do have every thing I need."*
—*Anonymous*

In this joyous season, these days of renewal of faith, and hope for tomorrow,
Days of tourists at the tree, of the sweet cold snow on Rockefeller Center;
I learn of the poet's passing, an e-mail from a mutual friend; I'd laughed with him,
Two weeks ago, the Orange Bear: where he read his stop-shorts, told us of the mail.

These bodies, we're told, are loaned to us, forty or sixty or eighty years; then we move on.
But while we're here, said Allen, we'll "*do the work…to ease the pain of living.*"
All this is temporary; all passes, fades; despite the daily struggles, money, work, love, survival:
May as well try to be useful, and happy, while we're all still here.

Crowded, this plane: all of us who still have bodies, the so many more who still come to visit;
Let us honor all our friends, we who cling to our wrappers, those who've left them behind.
This life in these bodies offers so much: more joy, more giving, more love, more possibility;
Our limitations: bodies, minds, souls, even Selves. Holy gifts: these, our limited lives, today.

**Chanukah. Christmas. Solstice. K'wanzaa.
Peace. Love, Light & Laughter:
Today.**

Graymoor - Croton, NY
December 2003

100.

(101) Holiday Poem: for Ryn

While America overeats,
      on the bird Ben Franklin wanted as our national symbol,

While we watch our football,
      deal as best we can with the dysfunction that is our families,

While our President stumbles through
      a blandly-written, blandly-thoughtout Thanksgiving message,

The Brooklyn poet will commune with her angels,
      will recharge, refresh, will prepare to ever-strengthen her art:

And I'll know the gratitude which comes from knowing that she's a friend.

Hawthorne, NY
November 2004

(102) Holiday Poem: 2004/5

New Year's Eve found me sick as a dog, alone, Fierce Grace becoming,
But better before dawn New Year's Day—eyes clearer, throat less inflamed, sinuses calmer.
Spent the night alone, watching Scorsese's great **Last Waltz**,
With The Band, and the stars—and Dylan, for the finale.

Reading D's **Chronicles**, his early 60's days in my cold wintry town,
D paying homage: Harold Arlen. Sinatra's *Ebb Tide.* So freakin' good.
The reviewer's great line: *"He's telling us: love and revere your masters,"*
As New Year's morning finds me naked, scribbling alone.

We can't ignore the November Disappointment, can't ignore Tsunami, Iraq,
But I left a message for her last night: Believe: it's your year. Mine. Ours.
We who've made it this far, we know the work that lies before us;
So much more yet to do. And just one day, each day, to do it all.

Sun's not up yet, New Year's morning; body slowly healing, old computer still working;
Every moment changes each of us, all of us. The good shall yet, in the end, triumph.

Croton-on-Hudson, NY
01.01.2005

102.

(103) Holiday Poem 2005

Years ago I was sure of who I was, who I wanted to be, even
Who I might yet become; these days, that surety's gone.
Mornings, evenings, days pass, tasks are completed, but
Now floating: what best to do before this time runs out?

That seems mind-stuff, a luxury, an entertainment,
There've been many choices, overlaid upon the givens; we do.
The country's still at war, the country's still so divided;
As I ride these east coast highways, I know I'm not alone.

I've kept my old vinyl, re-playing Dylan, Paul Simon, Paul Desmond;
The culture remains strong, though politics & economy seem shakier.
Snow fell early this year, large fat flakes onto hard NYC streets,
I watched, alone, from the 18th floor. Omen, perhaps; but omen of what?

Perhaps that hardships will come, yes, inevitably, but none insurmountable:
The country, the culture, the individual: so much work left, so much joy;

Growing, strengthening, into the New Year; into the New.

Croton-on-Hudson, NY
December 2005

(104) Holiday Poem: 2007

*"It's **supposed** to be fun!"*
—Lou Rawls

And Rawls is followed by Dizzy and James Moody, *"Swing Low, Sweet Cadillac,"*
Not only great jazz but great laughs too; and Mulligan's chosen as BGO's favorite baritone,
So, I'm guessing that maybe the Abe-ster's right—there is no death—the vibes just continue.

From my limited perspective, though: changes. Savannah in November is NY in early fall,
Maybe a cool evening breeze off the lake, a day or two of frost on morning windshields.
I fit in well here, homogenized America, but there's specific new joys, new discoveries:
The Confederate monuments.. The still-green squares, downtown. Tybee beach.

Six months here, I'm planning re-invention: again. Who I am, what I am; what I yet might become.
Dropped the wildest dreams, but dreams still live; collected music, words & images for 30+ years;
I surround myself with them, and there's always more, and newer: pleasures, without attachment.

Most people end up with partners; hasn't been that way for me. Not a bad thing, just the way it is;
There's work & laughter, friends & art, music & poetry; and always: opportunities; possibilities:
Service. These days, the New Yorker's in Savannah; seems a good place to be, these days;
Connections still strong. There's work, and there's fun, too: like capturing clouds at the beach.

Chanukah. Christmas. K'wanzaa. Solstice.
Love, Light and Laughter. Today.

Pooler, GA
November 2007

104.

(105) Cloud, Tybee

105.

(106) Holiday Poem: 2008
for Walt

Finally, the end of an error, as Gianni claimed back in 2004,
And maybe, some real change, beyond the obvious, may yet be rising.
Externals matter: like if you've just lost your job, or punched out that cop;
But for most, externals mostly continue. Change that matters must come from within.

For each of us must find our own silent, serene center,
Must quiet enough so accessibility is easy, and natural,
Must take action only when centered in that powerful, joyous place;
The world always changes. But the means must matter more than the ends.

I traveled much this year, Amsterdam, San Francisco, talking pearl pigments,
Drove my vacation, Georgia to Massachusetts, cruising in my old black Toyota,
Saw Emily's house in Amherst, Ava's museum in small-town Carolina:
Forget the tv talking heads: this country's strong, and good, and fair.

So, this is Christmas," sang John, years ago, and we hear him today, as
"Paperback Writer" also lives, background music, this Savannah barbeque joint.
Each individual matters, the country matters, we all live our continuing changes;
It's always been a great country. Each of us shall make it so, again.

Pooler – Savannah, GA
November – December 2008

(107) Holiday Poem: 2009

The turtle looks joy-filled, ecstatic, but he's probably swimming for his life;
From an e-mail, an unexpected gift; one of too-many saved, of many more discarded.
The other, the click of capturing colors, sunset on the lake: Pooler, September dusk;
A reflection: technology. This comfortable space, South Georgia. The choices I make, today.

Television gives us the nonsense of Olbermann and O'Reilly, the talking heads of the left and right,
But now the President has his war, as most seem to need. We pray for success, for completion.
The slowly-recovering economy affecting me only moderately; been lucky, my busy-ness still useful,
But there's a growing feeling for me to do more, to give more, to quiet, to change. To write: better.

The season, again, Thanksgiving to New Year's: the lesson of letting go, the silent, unalterable past,
Though a few sad souls do get stuck there. No, the way forward must be one of caring, of fulfillment:
With too little sleep, too little love, always with too much that needs to be done; but maybe not, really:
Desires are plentiful, powerful, serve us well; but sometimes it's just sweeter to float, downstream.

I'm always in the midst of it all, all of us are, always: the Holidays.
Have some fun! Gifts. Toys. Relax; kick back. It's the best thing we can do, today.

Pooler - Savannah, GA
December 2009

107.

(108) Holiday Poem: 2010

for Don Van Vliet
with thanks to Ret

I'm saddened by the tv news these days--my team lost--but more, we gave it away...
But politics've always been mostly theater--entertaining to watch, mattering little in my life.
In a dark cafe in Pooler, tv football behind me, James' *Country Road* warmly, through the speakers,
I wait for my burger & pineapple juice. Picked up a cold last week, maybe Toronto: it'll pass:
All things must pass.

The work goes on; the friends still seem to be around. Ossining Joe lost a kidney to cancer,
Linda retired; Jersey Joe's planning that, soon, Bill's being treated for PTSD...it goes on.
Me? I'll visit a customer, book the flight, prepare the samples and the sorta-new presentation;
Still so weak on discipline, I do honor my commitments. Usually, I show up; most of the time, on time,
It pays the bills, perhaps even more. It supports the rest of my life. It's good.

Always loved the two-faced god, Janus, able to look forward & backwards, the same time;
December's about holidays, Christmas, but January's our new beginning,
Even rivaling September, always, *"the true turning of the year,"*
As cold January approaches. But it is good, it is our time. We must, we can, seize this moment;
Transform our lives, the ways we want: our choices, our needs, desires, love.

In the cold days of our upcoming January, we're all given a new start,
And if the slates are not wiped snow-white, we're at least given a nod, an allowance, a bit of a pass:
Everything matters: our thoughts, dreams, words, actions, vibrations, all play a part, all of it matters;
We all need to change, to give, to grow, to contribute, to co-create, to all that's desired:
We get to be present--this new awakening, our own making. January, approaching soon.

Pooler, GA
December 2010

108.

(109) To All: the Poets, the Friends, All Those Who've Forgotten Me

It's time. Open our hearts,

No. Let me open my heart: to recognize, to accept
        the gifts
        the obligations
        this time, this changing place

From the warmth of this basement room, I remember all of you, salute all of you:

It's today. It's the only day we can act; the only time we can love.

Wilmington, DE
December 11

(110) Holiday Poem 2012

More than a year, now: Wilmington. I like it, it's real, almost diverse: a manageable size;
The basement apartment suits me more & more, though I've still leaves to pick up, albums to arrange;
The work's OK; "reorganization's" in the air—what that really means, no one seems to know (yet),
But I always smile as I return to my car, the recently-injured Toyota; I-95 south, back into Delaware.

It appears that we misinterpreted the Maya, cataclysm perhaps not, but major change always looms,
Though we expect it, rarely. Perhaps the President can create his own, triumphant legacy,
But the continuity of systems powerfully resists. Most of us, like me, just hope to continue;
Always need: back to basics, the empowerment of the individual—the true creator, the truest power.

I am, and feel, older than ever;   I've put on weight since Savannah, the knees hurt, the innards cry.
I wonder, more than ever, what I came here for;   so much seems undone, so much I'll miss, no doubt
I've been told,   just give it a couple more years, do the work, it ain't all over yet,
The Invisible Teachers say, *"the purpose of life is joy;"* I need to allow that, need to live that: better.

Can I yet change? Can the dulling daily struggle lapse into ease, comfort, joy; the welcome new day?
Seems against the grain, yet such remains possible. New day, new year, new life: relax. Float. Go.

For Christmas, Chanukah, Kwanza;
One Day at a Time. Today.

Wilmington DE – Philadelphia PA
November – December 2012

110.

(111) Holiday Poem: 2013

"Tell me, what is it you plan to do
with your one wild and precious life?"
--Mary Oliver

It hasn't been an easy year for many, been a tough year for some,
The sad obstructionists in Washington, railing, Obamacare's imperfection.
Give it two or three years, it'll change the basic fabric of our country,
It'll be a milestone, a legacy; the sad voices will fade, the nation richer, stronger, *healthier,* for it.

Twelve years ago, a surgeon offered me a knee replacement; I'm scheduled for February 2014.
I turned 60 this year, and though it's just a number, it seems still to matter (in a bad way):
Can't help but think mortality, what have I done, what's the little I've accomplished;
Maybe the Hindus are right, it's just another life, just dropping some karma. I'm still in the midst.

Joe's sculpture "Family" found its place in my home, though I always said, "Sweet Potatoes,"
But it's good art, pleasing to eye and spirit, placed just below the shelf for The Beats, my lineage.
I'm still on the job, Philadelphia these days, living in sweet, quiet Wilmington, and it's good;
I read my poems to other poets, and find connections, online, and in my past; these separated cities.

I love Mary's quote, and always, always fall short, but it's a bonfire for my spirit:
"All things are blessings, or blessings in disguise." A voice from my past. For the present. For more.

Wilmington, DE
December 2013

111.

(112) Holiday Poem: 2014
for David

The year started with the total left knee replacement, recovering alone, the basement apartment,
Eleven weeks away from the job; practicing walking; practicing retirement.   The goal was to walk
In Manhattan, finally did, December, puffing my way from Port Authority to the Hilton, poster duty;
Old & fat, but walking; as I'd wanted. Accomplishing the small, real goal; as other joints begin to cry.

We lost the fine actor in February, the OD on Jane Street, the depressed comic's suicide, August;
November brought us a Republican congress, and the sad guess that only gridlock will triumph.
August also, the young black man shot by the white cop, Ferguson, America; The resolution,
That story, far from over. Conversations and die-ins; a beginning. Toward an unknown end.

In December, a friend I'd known for 30 years, gone, the massive stroke; he never opened his eyes.
Waiting, the hospital, with *"his ex-wife & current child."* The body, the shell, a gift to medical science,
But I feel him floating around, these days. I sing of him at readings, talk this ongoing friendship,
The world is not a terrible place for the losses, it's a glorious place for them having been here.

When there's nothing else to do, we begin again, we trust, and love, for that gives us strength;
The holidays. heading toward a new beginning. 2015 awaits, new life in California; all this, continues:

Chanukah. Christmas. K'wanzaa. Solstice.
Today. Have a Happy Today.

Wilmington, DE
December 2014

112.

(113) Holiday Poem: 2016
for Jon Baylin

The news channels talking heads are gloating, or horrified:
The "unexpected" that came in November.
And most presidents will have their wars, they deserve them, or create them;
Trump starts with three; maybe he'll build on them more.

I worry for the country. Appalled by the choices, this billionaire cabinet
EPA and Education and Commerce and HUD; but we had
Eight years of W and the country still stands, though I shudder
To see the state of the nation, four years hence.

I myself do little. Continuing in an unhappy job, golden handcuffed,
But no; I lack the courage, the will to change. The remote and the recliner,
Conspiring against simple action. The comfortable wins, night after night,
And the poems that I might-have-written remain dormant; not dead, but silent. Difficult to salvage.

I no longer know why I'd write a poem; perhaps if asked, I'll give it a try. There was a time
This meant something. I long for the return, that revolutionary, transformative mind-set:

Not knowing how to create it again. I'm told it's in the doing; I want to be convinced.

Wilmington , DE
December 2016

113.

(114) Holiday Poem: 2017
for Jon Baylin

The Disrupter-In-Chief's still in Washington, the country divided into MSNBC & Fox,
It's the drama of the next tweet-in-waiting, maybe it'll be Jerusalem, maybe Pyongyang.
It's erratic, wrong-headed, the dismay of this would-be leader on the American stage,
But don't impeach; the other's a God-fearing darling of the cold conservative right,

And he'd truly be more diabolical, more desperate, more horrendous to us all.
Beyond politics: the cold air's swept into Wilmington, a little mid-December snow last week,
I seem to be moving away from the job. 19 years of pigments and lipsticks, of tech service and
Customer visits; the eternal goal: to sell one more kilo of pigment. My multinational blues.

I pulled hundreds of bottles off the shelves in my lab today, to be packed up, the new location;
The necessities, the difficulties, the requirements of the Company; yes, we'll move to the Navy Yard.
I tend to do what needs to be done, what seems the next right thing, but I'm tired, in deep fatigue;
Sadnesses of soul, of time & energy wasted, of six decades of a life of *"what should've been more."*

The natural disappointment of this senior citizen, but it wasn't all bad: I'd seen Paris, New Orleans,
Called NYC home for a while, even known a love or two, & let 'em all go & it's OK.
An optimistic new beginning awaits; I want to be of service, hope the pieces fall into place;
The poetry seemed removed, three years now; had to struggle to write these simple lines.

Though I'm always alone, there remains a handful of friends & family who still know me & care;
I'll wake tomorrow morning, know that life is still to be lived; that there's so much more for us to do.

Wilmington, DE
December 2017

114.

(115) Holiday Poem 2018
for Jack Kerouac and Brian Hassett

This the year I finally did it, finally gave up those golden handcuffs,
Struck out on my own, the basement apartment remaining the base,
Rooms filled with words & music, now more time to read & listen to them all;
I've retired, left those multinational blues behind; not looking back, not even once.

Well, what do I do with my time, now that time stretches deep into the small numbers of the night,
Usually I'm still up at 4 am, tv, videos, the old desktop still cookin', sleeping away mornings;
I show up more at those 12-step rooms, managing my addictions, staying unscathed, just for today,
I show up & sit with Clyde, 92, Parkinson's, just hanging on, dozing in the recliner; waiting for the end.

And my tv is filled with MSNBC, the few glances at FOX disappoint, and frighten,
And though they call it a blue wave, the Tweeter-in-Chief still reigns, still sadly in command.
But I trust in the goodness of this country, in its people, neither red nor blue but American,
As the chill wind whips into Wilmington, winter approaching; cutting through our thin coats & scarves.

Remembering & honoring the old god Janus, knowing both the year before, the year-to-come:
Now healthy, newly-bright, clear, inspired; alone, on this new road. Optimistic as all hell.

Wilmington. DE
November 2018

115.

IN THE MIDST OF IT ALL:

SELECTED POEMS

2000 - 2001

For David;

For Charlie;

For Chris;

Who've each helped me more

Than any of them can ever know.

Thanks.

AUTHORS' NOTE

In mid-1998, while unemployed and spending too much time and money at the casinos in Atlantic City, I found a book called **The Lazy Man's Guide to Riches**. I never actually finished the book—too lazy, I suppose—but one of its suggestions that I did take was to make a list of goals and put them in the form of already having achieved them. Goal four (of seven) was:

"I write poems to give myself pleasure and to help myself grow.
I enjoy disseminating my poems."

In a culture that's increasingly visual and less and less verbal, I continue to write the poems. In a culture that measures success primarily in monetary terms, I hold on to my day job, because I still believe that my poetry won't (yet) give me the kind of financial comfort that I want. But I do continue writing my poems, and I read them wherever and whenever I can. There's a very healthy, lively, vibrant poetry scene in New York, ranging from the slam poets at the Nuyorican and the Bowery Poets Clubs to the more staid Shelley Society and the Poet's Society of America, with venues like the Orange Bear and the Cranberry Café somewhere in between. There is a community of poets here; we write, we read, and, for the most part, we support one another.

This is a work-in-progress, as all work really is. It's also my attempt to disseminate my poems, to put them in a form in which others can see (judge, use, or enjoy) them. The book is in roughly chronological order, covering the period of February 2000 to December 2001. It begins with plans for a business trip to Europe and ends in the days following September 11. At its best, it's an honest portrayal of one man's internal life, in the midst of our American culture, 2000 - 2001.

If you're reading this now, you've probably got at least a passing interest in poetry—in fact, you're probably writing your own. Take a look—maybe these'll work for you. If not, just let 'em go. Write your own; write what's true for you. It'll be a poem, if that's what you want it to be.

"Sometimes, you really have to write the poem
In order to discover what you really wanted to say."

Keep writing. I will, too. And I'll look for your poems, as well.

PL, Newark, NJ - Los Angeles, CA
23 March 2002

(123) The Trip: Before

The semi-frozen Hudson, the purple Palisades beyond,
Bright Sunday afternoon, early, cars speeding north, Route 9.
Minimizing carbs, sausage parm, onion rings, putting aside the bread:
Café au lait. With Paris, five days away.

Preparation, yes. Fear & anxiety, yes. Readiness? Maybe.
The process exists. Entering. Accepting.
Anticipation just another thought; time changes:
Here & now will be Air France. Here & now will be the Parisian cafes.

Need to cover bills, need to check travel guides,
Need to quiet, to center, to internally prepare
The corporate obligations, the many actions to be taken:
The letting go of results. Living the process, letting this happen.

Turning my will & life over; the tickets in my hand, the quiet, almost-relaxed smile:
To move forward, to challenge, to succeed; following, humbly: this, my given path.

Croton - Hawthorne, NY
February 2000

123.

(124) Working: The Tour

Paris as dawn breaks; the road to Orleans
Lingerie ads, quiet mandolin on CD
Swimming through, struggling with, a language not my own,
The day breaking, the thick clouds: the gray Parisian drizzle.

Le raison d'etat: the customer visits,
Scientists as salesmen, chemists as *explaineurs,*
Being introduced as *"the American experts,"* cringing a bit,
Yet showing the slides, showing the samples; French women, Japanese firm.

The first presentation: noting its imperfections,
Perhaps an overkill of samples, but they need to be shown.
High tension wires, transformers, the highway to the gig;
81 kilometers to Orleans. Late afternoon, Breton.

So it is Chanel, and Yves St. Laurent, and L'Oreal, and the heavy rain back to Paris;
Les Mousketaires Americaine. The Bismuth show. On the road.

Paris
February 2000

124.

(125) "Flying Home"
for Tammy

The teaching is that of openness
The more you reveal, the more others feel free to reveal
Strangers meeting two seats away, Frankfurt to Newark,
The gifts of comfort, relaxation, trust: seeds warmly, easily planted.

Too long in Europe, way too long in Deutschland,
Last days only marking time, missing the humor, German tv comedy;
A worthwhile trip, perhaps a beginning, perhaps the sales will rise,
But personal contacts made, through the continent. Now stronger; now connected.

Still too close to understand, the multilayered experience still too fresh,
Yet the work was solid, strong presentations, even the work in the Darmstadt lab;
Living the culture changes, learning all that comes with *"Das is nicht in orden;"*
But wanting to work together. Wanting growth, coordination. For the company. For myself.

The icing on the cake, a sweet chance meeting, the long welcome flight home;
The journey over, finally, safely, successfully. Another step: the long road ahead.

Frankfurt—Newark
March 2000

125.

(126) Vision

I'd met her on a retreat, ten years ago now,
Skin a smooth dark brown, sleek, maybe the hips a little large,
But accessible; so it seemed. Big broad smile, quiet intelligence,
My lust saw possibilities. Disguised in sensitivity, in spirit; dating, the 90's.

A phone call to Brooklyn, the odd invitation, a healing Mass,
Catholic church, Greenpoint; an unlikely first date.
My hand in her hand, checking out the stained glass, waiting, the show to start;
Fifty feet above me, floating, in her yellow housedress: my mother, two years dead.

My Jewish mother frowning, shaking her head, wagging her finger,
Clearly upset, her only son, for her the wrong place,
The Jew, the wrong pew, lusting the *schwartze shiksa*
My mother: disappointed. Saddened. The image gone--but real.

Stunned; though knew this was truth. Later, we broke up, wasn't meant to be,
But my mother's shade watching, knowing, some other plane

Clear: a vision. A gift. A living connection.

NYC - Las Vegas
March 2000

126.

(127) It's OK To Go Gentle, Into That Good Night

without apologies to DT

It's OK to go gentle, into that good night,
The body's a limited vehicle, age's frailty conquers every man;
Dignity, acceptance--the dying of the light.

Wise men, who won the games, who scaled the heights,
Success, power, toys--the emptiness of wind, the solitude of sand;
It's OK to go gentle, into that good night.

Good men, who gave of themselves, who lived through right
Work, who struggled past goodness, who really gave a damn;
Dignity, acceptance--the dying of the light.

Wild men who partied black nights, gray dawns tight,
Who laughed, loved, all appetites, all pleasures at hand;
It's OK to go gentle, into that good night.

Grave men, who accept inevitability, who've gone beyond the fight,
Trusting unseen belief, sad darkness giving the bright new land;
Dignity, acceptance--the dying of the light.

And you, my father, alone, the yellow cab, the theater lights,
Remember the love, your only son; the unfinished business, as best we can;
It's OK to go gentle, into that good night.
Dignity, acceptance--the dying of the light.

Westchester County, NY - NYC
May - July 2000

127.

(128) Poem of Desire

"Let go / of wanting / all of it"—PL

Two years ago I wrote down all that I wanted out of life. One page. Seven goals.
    Clear. Concise. True (still).
Copies of that page are still on my wall at home, they're folded into my ever-carried
    datebook, they remain silent in a file at work. Always accessible,
I keep 'em around me, close, I want to sharpen my awareness of my vast desires,
    want to remain focused, want always to remember that
These are what I want. To accept that I want all of these. To want. To accept my
    own wanting. And, of course, I want also: to let go. To let go of wanting.
    All of them. To let go of wanting all of them.

It's about freedom, clarity, lightness, about living in the moment, floating,
    flowing easily downstream, it's about the easier, softer way,
    the right way, the way of discipline, the way of achievement,
    the way of being
The way of just being

Taking right action to realize these goals
Finding levels of success, of failure
New moment; new moment; new moment;
Choosing not to take action; choosing waiting

Practicing breathing
Practicing waiting
(Though both breathing and waiting are taking actions)

Barnes & Noble coffee bar
Iced coffee, Saturday afternoon
The ego-vision of publication
Of joining these masses, these billions of words, this very familiar place
    (which is why I come to this very familiar place; this place that I love)

128.

From the Gita, Krishna's command
"Do what you do, but dedicate the fruits of your action to Me."

Love
Money
Work
Poetry
Addictions
Health
G-d

I have been given: so very much

I want.
I want.
I want.

The ever-moving present:
I am.

Ossining - Cortlandt - Croton, NY
June - July 2000

(130) Barnes & Noble Poem

for Erica

When I'm blocked, I come here
(Though "blocked" gives too much credit to the fact that I'm simply not writing)
But I like it here
Though the air conditioning is on too high for this damp August night

Like a gambler wearing the same lucky t-shirt or choosing the same dealer or the same
     amount to bet,
Or noting the position of the moon or the stars or the proper hexagram of the *I Ching*,
There was a dry spell for months, the poems were stuck, I was between jobs & she was still
     in my life & the writing
Wasn't happening. At the Barnes & Noble in Princeton I wanted it so much, I thought of
     the death exercise & tried to write of it, I became empty, I just let the words flow,
     I sipped at my coffee & wrote & read & reread & corrected & I wasn't even
     "creating" it, it was just that the poem was just happening & I was just there,
My hand moving with the moving pen, the black ink, the words appearing on the white paper,
     the coffee being sipped, the air conditioning still on too high

And when it was finished there was a poem. Not a finished poem, no, not yet, but a good
     first draft, and it looked like a poem, it sounded & felt like a poem,
     & I knew it was a poem & G-dammit I cried,

Don't know if from relief or ego or just the G-d-damned getting it out, but I did weep,
And now that poem's around & about & living its own life, and it's OK. And I had that
     experience, one day, between jobs, the Barnes & Noble in Princeton,
     a late Thursday afternoon, July, a couple of years ago.

So now I leave the Paramount Theater in Peekskill after the excellent but ill-advised gambling movie
     with all the energy & excitement & anxiety of the addict,
And no, I don't aim my car for the Connecticut casinos but rather for the B&N in Cortlandt,
     that rare spot in Northern Westchester where at 10 pm on a Saturday night I can get a coffee
     and look at books by Frank O'Hara and Robert Bly and Donald Hall
And I order the large coffee and find the empty table in the back, I pull out the tools of the writer
     and I just let the words flow
The coffee's good. But the AC is still on too high.

It's an honest poem. It's OK. It's what I do.

Cortlandt - Croton, NY/August 2000

130.

(131) Poem: On Receiving Advice to Become Bankrupt

I randomly open a book of Rumi's poems and the mystic's advice is, *"Die now, die now…"*
I can only hope that he's writing metaphorically

She walks swiftly through the stacks, clearly intent only on the bathroom,
Perhaps twenty-three, fine, fastmoving breasts & ass.
I'm sure there's so much more to her than that, but the 20/20's are clouded;
Desires—all of 'em!—which can't, or won't, be satisfied. Love. Money. Work. All of it.

Snippets of wisdom stored in my head
Don't seem to help much when the Visa bills are due

"The best thing to do with a bill is to pay it."
I've tried that. I'm still doing it. Don't know if it's working or not.
In this, my quick-fix culture, the long-term struggle, the dimly-lit path, is despised
Yet I'm drawn to that difficulty, clearly before me. This path I've created; this way, today.

Arbitrarily, another book. Stafford: *"It is important that awake people be awake."*
I seem to resist the best advice given to me. Am I not yet awake? How deeply do I sleep?

Is it simply pride, or Self, or ego? Is it fear, or guilt, or shame? Is it failure?
Is it hiding under responsibility's cloak? Does it really matter, in all that does matter?
The long drives back from AC or Foxwoods, beaten, beaten, beaten again,
The price, which remains to be paid. The price, which can't be wished away.

I'll finish the coffee, leave the table, go home and write the checks;
Nothing finite can't be obtained. Choosing the darker path; trusting, this painful process.

Cortlandt - Hawthorne, NY
August 2000

131.

(132) The Night I Kissed David Drake

"The truth will set you free,
but it'll piss you off first."—DD

Hadn't expected it to be the *premiere*
Soft gray summer Saturday, visiting the old haunts,
23rd Street for the necessary haircut, meeting the older gentleman who likes his boys naked
Both of us checking out the twenty-something boys & girls at the trendy new coffee bar

D. was meeting his "nephew," or so he said, so simply a link to the future, or maybe not,
Back on the street, where to go—? No desire to return early to the suburbs of the north,
A meeting, a movie, a reading—? Walk to St. Mark's, perhaps the calendar, some direction,
But nothing but the joys of the crowded streets, the free *Voice* for listings: dinner, Thai; alone.

Checking the paper, *"The Night Larry Kramer Kissed Me,"* Screening Room, 4, 6, 8, 10.
"It'll never play Westchester," the same movies making the rounds, the suburban multiplexes,
Needing the City for diversity, for true depth of culture. Waiting outside, the rain, the umbrellas,
The audience: 90% NYCGM: the right crowd. And finally: the movie. The film of theater.

One man, one voice: one gay man's story. 16 in Balamer, the gym, the clubs, the plague;
We laughed the right places, remembered our young men dying, howled at future dreams,
His story, our story, gay American life, end of the twentieth century, and still further,
Taking our full place, the fabric of this world. Making our contributions—choosing our paths.

The director & the writer/star spoke afterward, another level of connection, our community:
The line of men embracing, kissing; moving on. Political, sexual, human: we need to fight:

But more: we need to love.

NYC - Croton-on-Hudson, NY
July 2000

132.

(133) The Days of Awe

As mood swings go, it wasn't much

From the worked-for high of the completion of the book & the reading on Sunday

To the sexual unavailability
To the formulas & processes giving ugliness
To the required phone call, with only a message left
To the continuing automotive paranoia
To the organizing of the meeting, the possibility of the merger
To the speed of the race home to beat the curfew, & hearing only busy signals
To the accounting, the money at month's end, remaining, deep, that desperate valley
To the unnecessary worry waking me, angry, from my restless, troubled dreams
To the formulas & processes still giving ugliness, relief not yet in sight
To the evening alone, with hope for calmness & rest
To the four-a.m. wakefulness, rest denied again,
To the self-created anxiety, the workplace,
To the reluctant meeting

Where I spoke of the pain of living & how I seem to be facing, accepting & dealing with it

To the bologna sandwich on raisin bread in front of the television set, alone
To the wrenching tears from that place of pain, too-deep inside
To the old, familiar feelings of uselessness, & self-doubt
To know that they're lies:
To reaffirm the trust, the direction

To believe that these struggles will yield growth & usefulness
To accept that all pains & joys of this life will only move me forward
To become aware of the rising & falling of the moods, of the breath, of how this works

The cycle: from the high to the low to the break; a difficult, necessary four bitter days:
To watch, as from a distance: this play; this life; my life: today.

Hawthorne, NY/October 2000

133.

(134) Poem: for Chris

To serve is to be as water
The task is to fit yourself to the dimensions of need

You will give away only what you own
If you own anger, you shall give that to others
If you own calmness, others will see that too

The fallen brown leaf, the surface of the waters
Neither wanting or needing; simply being

The gifts and obligations of consciousness
The choices of being swayed, the many moods & passions
The return to recognition, the task: of quietness, of centering

Struggles and suffering: necessities, this game, this life
The destroying fire of growth. The cleansing trials, toward surrender.

Hawthorne, NY
November 2000

(135) Poem: for the New Kid on the Block

for Parand

Odd how we live our lives, the changes we go through
We put our desires out into the universe & the universe responds
Maybe not exactly in the way we wanted, maybe not in the way we think we need
Maybe just in the way it's supposed to be

So easily, so freely, I can give out advice
But I give away freely, only what I own:

> *"Wear your work - and your life - like a loose garment."*
> *"Trust your heart, your gut, and your mind (in that order)."*
> *"Don't take life so seriously…it ain't gonna be permanent."*
> *"In the midst of pain, remember the importance of laughter."*
> *"90% of life is just showing up."*
> *"Show up. Listen. Remember to laugh."*
> *"Don't hold on. Let things pass."*
> *"Just do the next right thing."*
> *"Some things are beyond your control. You'll still be called on them."*
> *"Take the heat; don't take it to heart."*
> *"To sell well is to lead. To lead well is to serve."*
> *"Just relax. Enjoy this part of your journey."*

You're here with us, you're there in the golden west,
You're alone, 3K miles from your home in Hawthorne; you're not alone.
You're here because we need you to show the products, to speak for us, to sell for us;
We're here for you, fiber optics & modems, samples & quotes & data; we will support you:

As you will succeed and grow, in this new service; in this, your new work.

Ossining - Croton-on-Hudson, NY
January 2001

135.

**(136) The Sopranos: A Pantoum
(After the Second Season Finale)**

It's only a tv show, but we do love it so
We root for Tony, 'cause he plays by the rules
Proud father, loyal soldier, adulterer, murderer
"But no one gets whacked who don't deserve to get whacked"

We root for Tony, 'cause he plays by the rules
De facto boss, with Junior hounded by the Feds
"But no one gets whacked who don't deserve to get whacked"
It's all about the business; it's all about the family

De facto boss, with Junior hounded by the Feds
Big Pussy dead, Richie Aprile dead, even Jackie Junior dead
It's all about the business; it's all about the family
Meadow dumped, betrayed, now drinking heavily, her grief

Big Pussy dead, Richie Aprile dead, even Jackie Junior dead
Proud father, loyal soldier, adulterer, murderer
Meadow dumped, betrayed, now drinking heavily, her grief
It's only a tv show, but we do love it so.

Ossining - Croton, NY
April - May 2001

136.

(137) Bat Mitzvah Poem
for Nikki

Child of your parents, of struggles and suffering and laughter and jazz,
Child of our City, of Rockaway sands and hard NYC concrete,
Child of the program, learning how to glide through these days with a swimmer's easy grace;
Child: who will not be child, forever. The early teens; this new beginning.

The ritual: as it's been since Moses gave us the Law,
The people of the Book; our rich history: survival past oppressors.
To take your place today as a full, responsible member of the tribe;
A new beginning, this day. To leave childish things behind.

And maybe it'll be that the religion won't be your heart,
Maybe you'll sit zazen, chant dark foreign blessings, feel the spirit in other ways,
Maybe your Jewish roots won't matter much, maybe your own way will differ;
Maybe you'll always know, someway, you're a Jew. Maybe you'll be proud of your Bat Mitzvah.

Just another day, a warm spring day, East 22nd Street, NYC;
Your work. Your family. Your day. Today.

Croton, NY - NYC
May 2001

137.

(138) Poem for Andy

This is how he looks, only days before he dies:
Toothless mouth open, eyes closed, lying in a hospital bed, his own bedroom
Breathing…still. Seemingly resting comfortably.
Every once in a while, a throat-gurgle, a cough
Perhaps a swab of the syrupy orange liquid to moisten the lips, the tongue, the mouth

Andy at 86, 53 years married, two children, four grandchildren
His wife at the church this morning, the youngest granddaughter's christening,
Pictures describing his lifetime on every wall of the modest apartment.
Early May 2001, 1010 WINS quietly from the kitchen,
His chest moving gently with his breathing. He appears to be resting; comfortably.

This is how the process works, not for all, but for Andy, here, now.
The startled sound of a gurgle. I jump; should I give the moisture, the spongy swab?
It passes; we go with the flow. He relaxes. It happens again, again I jump, ready; I wait;
Again it passes. Mouth wide open; not really awake; not really asleep;
The red LED on the feeding pump. The IV stand next to the bed.

This the worst of it, the waiting.
When action is minimized, when there's little to do now but wait.
The Hospice movement: a way of thinking, of gentling, into death.
The goal: to maximize comfort. For Andy. For all those around him.
To die. Peacefully. Surrounded by family. In your own bed. At home.

A bedroom, an apartment in White Plains, NY.
Floral wallpaper; a wooden crucifix on the wall.
A man I'd never met before today rests in bed, while Spring dances joyously, outside.
Not the majesty of death, not the full orchestration, not the booming cannons;
But the quiet; the simplicity. Two men, sharing this space; this moment; only this moment.

White Plains - Croton, NY
May 2001

138.

(139) Lipstick
after Mark Doty

This is not about the final form, not the familiar imagery
      Rich; warm; wet; shiny…seductive
      Bordeauxs to purples to corals to Barbie-doll pinks
The promise; the tease; the deliberately hot ads

This is the lab, science and art in Janus form
      The oft-repeated preparations
      R&D to marketing to sales, the necessary triad
The rhythm of business; sweet when they all work together

The great solid mass, the yellow-bland base
      Candelilla, carnauba, the long-chain paraffinics
      The new wet ester, amazing payoff, surprising coverage,
The ubiquitous expressed oil: ricinoleic. The staple; the classic.

But the base is just the wood, this stage: the color's the performance:
      Clean organic reds, sixes, sevens, orange, blue,
      Iron oxides, nanometer-thin TiO_2, micas from Arizona, from India,
For pearlescence: pearlescence. The bias of the poet; his pleasure, as well.

The many suppliers serving this, our complex industry,
      All screaming: New; Different; Better. (Cheaper, too.)
      Feeding the demands of this market, the masses, the elite:
And competition, seemingly gentle, does burn; it does burn.

But in those tiny supplier's labs, crowded, hundreds of sample jars,
      The formulators begin: the next new project; the magic.
      Splendid lipsticks, two-tone palettes:
Pushing the envelope: formulating the lipstick.

Detroit - Newark - Croton, NY
August - October 2001

(140) Poem: for Joe

I give you this scene, this image:

An iron railing, wild rose bushes in bloom, a gentle river breeze, their perfume;
It rained heavily last night; we spoke, this morning. Your decision:
Not to drive the too-open bridge. Not to visit Westchester, today.

It rained through mid-day, I was lazy, drank too much coffee, read, did laundry,
Listened to Harry Chapin, Emmylou Harris and the Dukes of Dixieland;
The afternoon passed. Now the bright sunshine, China Pier,

Leaning on the black painted railing, watching a hardworking bee,
The yellow pollen of the wild rose sticking to its legs, busy, focused,
Concentrating on the work—doesn't even know, or care, that it's Sunday—

The view is the river, green hills almost meeting; the sound, the lapping waters,
The howl of a Metro North train off to the east, heading for the City,
Bear Mountain Bridge nearly invisible, the sun-haze distance.

The hardships of our lives won't disappear, a single Sunday by the river,
But it does give a measure of centering, of quiet; it keeps us going, just a bit longer

The sun's strong now. Had it been so this morning you'd be here with me,
Listening to the old folkies; listening to the river. Didn't even go to the concert, today,
But did come down to the river's edge. To hear its sweet music. To think about you.

We deal with what we've been given. *"Life on life's terms."* We deal.
Families dissolve. Old bitterness. Money hassles. Meanness of spirit.
The recognition: that accidents of birth don't make for real families.

You have beauty, strength, art in your spirit. You have laughter and joy,
Ease and goodness. You can give love, and take love, and share your love.
There is purpose, and meaning, and value to your life. Your life matters;

Your life does matter.

(141) Poem: for Joe (cont.)

A man, a woman, two children, the pier; a Sunday afternoon, the young family;
Perhaps that role, that husband, that father, won't be mine, this life. Nor yours, this life.
We accept what we'd been given. We find love where it's true, for us.

We grow. We do our work. We live. We love. We create our own lives:
"These, our unique expressions."   The Spirit, living gloriously. In me. In you.

Peekskill - Croton, NY
June 2001

(142) AC

Choosing to disregard the warnings of friends & family,
But needing this. As the break; away from the recent work-filled, unbalanced life.

Arrived alone, the seaside city, early afternoon, gray Tuesday.
Found the right spot. Played well—no fear allowed—and walked, 880 up.
A comp for the buffet dinner. Check-in to the room, comped. Reservation for the show, comped.
And a walk on the boardwalk, all the way to the end: Showboat. Playing. Another 575 up.

Not in town four hours, 13 new Franklins in the pocket. The easy walk back;
New porn slipped into my overnight bag. The tower room, the large tub, the ocean view.
Time to taste, too much: steak & shrimp, chowder, egg rolls, latkes, rice pudding & chocolate mousse,
Coffee at the Legends, impressions of Madonna, Streisand, and always--ending with The King.

The belly sated, the mind amused, time to go back to work.
And here I stayed too long at her table, dropping 2, 2, 2—600 fast of their money,
But still ahead, so what did it matter? The luck was gone, my 20's beaten by her 21's,
Over & over again, couldn't win a thing all night. Back to the room, hurting—but still, 300+ up.

Alone the hotel room, sexual pleasures, alone—this is how I live, this life.
Woke early; hit the tables by 9. 9:30 some 400 down, Park Place,
To the other side, another deuce out the wallet—some recovery. Back in the room, still net 350 up;
Bathe, shower, pack, checkout by noon. Coffee, bagel & a bear claw for breakfast. And back to it.

And here's the heart of it—wanting the money, but it's not about money, not about the damned money,
The playing. The belief—that everything can change. *The dream world of the compulsive gambler.*
And the cards turned against me, as always. And the winnings were gone, and so was the stake.
And the credit card. The debit card. The credit card, again. Pushing it, now.

Stopped. Walked. 380 left in the pocket. Some 1400 down; the terrible cards.
A walk on the beach: I know I should go home. Don't wanna gamble any more, ain't gonna win;
Walk to Resorts. And what does it matter now, 1400 or 1700. Don't even wanna play;
But don't wanna go home the loser. Find the seat, lose a little, nearly all gone…then I start to win.

Slowly at first, but then I've a little breathing room & I'm rolling…betting 65, 85, more, and winning:
Still a long way back. Count the quarters as she shuffles, three stacks, 42 quarters, I could leave now,
Only be some 7 down. But now I'm chasing it…& the next shuffle I count 33. And the clock ticks on.
Plan was to leave, drive home, wake for work at 7, tomorrow. But I stay—and I don't recover.

Cash in some 80 bucks, the same in the wallet; beaten, the winnings to the losings, & letting it go;
"Coulda; woulda; shoulda." The song of the loser. And loser is what I am, what I set myself up for;
But it's OK. Not what I'd'a wished for: it is what I got. It's my own action, I got this, I can own this;
Nothin' left to do but drive back home. A three-hour drive home, without a break…and it's over.

'Course it's not over, back at work the next day, 29 e-mails, 10 voice-mails, too much to do…
By mid-afternoon I'm snapping at co-workers. The bureaucracy; the right-back-to-it. In my face.
It's a payday; at home I'll write the checks, pay the bills; again, I'll make it, I will survive;
But in front of the meeting, I lose it; I curse, I scream. The shoelace breaking; the living on this edge.

I don't regret it, I lived like a rich man for 24 hours, then I had to pay; I can accept that;
I do regret snapping, screaming, the stupidity toward others. Unprovoked; but for my own mind.
Days later, bored, depressed, a quiet, dull anger…it ain't the money, it's the misdirection, the waste:
These choices that I make, today. The sadness, the emptiness—wasting this precious gift, this life.

We go on, we wait for moods to pass, we trust, we know that they will;
We show up. We fuck up. We change. It does get better.

Croton -Hawthorne, NY
June 2001

(144) On Hearing: the Poet on the Radio
for Ryn

1.
You'd think that the poem should be about Brooklyn,
Maybe the Brooklyn that lies to itself, calling itself the 4th largest city in America
(I remember that sign, the Belt Parkway, just after coming off the Verrazanno Bridge);
Because it's not a city, it's a part of a city, but if it were a city it'd be the 4th largest in America
So, it's a case of melting-pot denial, I suppose
Which is uncommonly prevalent within the City of New York

2.
I don't mind being on e-mail mailing lists. I found out this morning that you were on the radio,
Dialed the old lab-radio to the station of the City of New York and heard what I thought was
Cole Porter creakily singing his own words, telling us that nowadays, *"Anything Goes,"*
Or maybe it was Noel Coward, but I think it was Porter; anyway it had to be eighty years old,
Hardly a fitting introduction to your words, the words of this Brooklynite by inclination
But that's what I heard, and then I heard your prose, your poetry. Your unique sense of place, of mind.

3.
We were neighbors in the East Village, yet never met. I lived above a funeral home,
12th Street and Avenue A, from the time Andy left the city & moved to Connecticut to get married,
'Til the time the bridge-&-tunnel street-pissers became the prevalent force in the neighborhood,
'81 to '97. And commuted into Jersey. I spent long years in the belly of that mythical beast,
The heart of Oz, and don't regret a thing. *That sounds so dramatic:*
There's much that I'd've changed. But I lived it; I own it; it's part of what makes me me, today.

4.
Sometimes it seems such a small, tight, incestuous circle, the writers, the readers, our Circuit, today.
We keep the backbiting to a minimum—out loud, anyway. Bad form, y'know. Gotta go for win/win.
But we all want to publish, want others to know our work, want approval, we all want our 15 minutes…
Most of us know, or suspect a bit, how silly it all is: writing at all, writing poetry especially! Yet:
We are tied, to Whitman, to Rumi; to Kerouac, to Poe; to the so many others, all now forgotten;
We write. We sing of ourselves, sing our times, sing the complex mazes illuminating our minds…

    And sometimes—like gerbils—we eat our young.

Hawthorne, NY/July 2001

144.

(145) Poem: With a Theme by Ellison

"The tribunal will not ask, 'Why were you not Moses?'
But they may well ask, 'Why were you not Harry Ellison?'"
—HE, Brooklyn, NY, July 01

One alone, in the midst of the crowd: Atlantic Avenue, Brooklyn
One alone: only a face in the crowd. But unique, uniquely myself,
Uniquely identifiable. Fingerprints. DNA. Social Security number. Poetry:
The work, which belongs uniquely, to me. Sharing: with all those who care to listen.

We begin with the given: imposed, the arrangements of ACTG's;
Nature **and** nurture. The cruelty of children, the schoolyard,
Early dynamics; establishing patters. The victim; the bullies;
The many schools. A measure: successes; a measure; failures.

Free-floating Fear, the constant companion: compensating, as per this culture:
Booze. Drugs. Mania. And the dead ends they all offered.
Therapy.   The beginnings of recovery: a working, workable structure,
Leading to growth: the Spirit. Taking these small steps, this simple, difficult path. My path.

The day job always, always necessary, this time around. A requirement of this culture,
This culture of commerce, the buying, the selling. My role: to help them buy.
Writing formulas: lipsticks. Pressed powders. Nail lacquers. Technical support.
This business of color, a gift, to the poet. And checks are deposited, twice-monthly. Directly.

For the spirit to breathe we must love the day job, the many hours spent,
But so much more fills these days, these nights. The creation of a new poem,
The bittersweet search for love; more, for its easier-accessible imitation.
The giving: service. The listening: silence. The brilliance: available to all.

Not a patchwork quilt, it's all one thread, all one fiber,
These many avenues, these many collaborations; these blessings: this life.
The choices I make; the ever-deeper, deeper, deeper surrender:
To shine mine own light. To share it freely: with all who care to listen.

Brooklyn - Rockaway Beach, NY/July 2001

145.

(146) Desiderata Poem

From jaw-wrenching abscesses to Kaposi's Sarcoma to being gored in Pamplona to
　　　suffocating 'neath a pink pillow when you're four months old

From an hour on the subway to breaking through the last traffic jam to stepping blindly into
　　　the empty elevator shaft to walking a brisk eight minutes from your bedroom to your work-desk

From the misty almost-rain of the tropical island to new snowboarding with your best friend's lover
　　　to drinking the young widow under the table to hundred dollar bets in Vegas, rolling

From here to there
From this to that
From me to you to her to him and then back again, to me
And I have to choose, where to go, what to do, what shall we do, what shall I do, today

They do say that there's no choice,
It's only apparent choice, that's what they say
The heart the mind the eye the brain the hand the mouth the cock the soul the connection
Beyond the elements of composition; the whole infinitely greater than the sum of its parts

From springtime in the burning-green veldt to winter in the dark rain of cobblestoned Paris
　　　to summer in the arms of she-who-must-be-obeyed to autumn alone, accepting
　　　your own death

From English as a second language to boardrooms of decision-making capitalists to
　　　slaughterhouses and birthday parties to just another day in America

From all we've needed to all we've asked for to all we've dreamed of to all that we have, today;

Here;
Now.
Unimaginable;
Accessible.

Croton-on-Hudson, NY
July 2001

146.

(147) When the Darkness Sweetly Beckons

for J; via Charlie

In those bleak moments, when the darkness sweetly beckons,
When the only sensible thing seems to burn it all, to end it all, for now, forever;
The necessary work is to deny that lie. The real work before us: to choose life, over death.

Deep in her own shadows, couldn't hear, couldn't know: the depths of love, so much, so many;
Desperately seeking relief, stepping outside the barred window, to fly, to shatter;
In those bleak moments, when the darkness sweetly beckons

To walk the Atlantic shore, August, the crescent moon's moving reflection,
To wait: to want that same moon, that same reflection; cold February, still alive:
The necessary work is to deny that lie. The real work before us: to choose life, over death.

So hard to live, this culture of speed and dollars and irony and surrender
So hard to make it, failed relationships, lost jobs; always the loneliness; always the terror;
In those bleak moments, when the darkness sweetly beckons

But it's possible to sit on a Sunday park bench, to feel the August sun warm your living skin,
Summers of soft vanilla ice cream, trumpets, car horns, and the tiniest possibility of love before I die:
The necessary work is to deny that lie. The real work before us: to choose life, over death.

The mystery, the diversity, the simplicity: runners on a pier, drummers on a dashboard,
The ease of the tourists, the promenade; the ferry. The City, beyond, alive: waiting: *for you:*
In those bleak moments, when the darkness sweetly beckons,
The necessary work is to deny that lie. The real work before us: to choose life, over death.

Brooklyn – Hawthorne, NY
August 2001

147.

(148) After 9-11

"You've got a hand and a voice
and you're not alone,
Brother, that's all you need to know."
—Phil Ochs

1.
"And it came to pass that the terror rained down from the skies. And the horror was unimaginable.
And the stench of death filled the city streets. And the glacier-slow recovery began."

A month passes. And two. And three. And the process continues:
Retaliation. The Afghan air show, watched on American television. And our continuing anger.

As one American plane drops bombs, and another American plane drops food. Surreal.

2.
And the mood of the country is the mood of the City. And it's anger, of course it's anger,
But more: it's defiance. Our innocents; our heroes: shall not go unavenged.

We ask ourselves what to do now, where to go from here. It's simple: we do what we do:
Politicians talk; soldiers fight; accountants count; sales writes orders; customer service listens;

We continue. We bear the unbearable. We pray. And more: we know that we shall endure.

3.
The accepted inevitability: change. The color of the leaves along the Taconic, as it's always been,
Thanksgiving. The Holiday season, again. Christmas. And the end of this dark, dark year.

All of us are changed by this. And all remain cursed with these times, yet oddly blessed as well:
Blessed with renewal of commitment: the strength, the goodness; the possibility that is still America.

Painfully relearning this schoolbook lesson, in a new, grisly way. Re-creating: our old/new America.

4.
Each of us must still choose, now, today: a single act of kindness, or bravery, or courage
Multiplied by a million, or ten million, or three hundred million

The power of this country remains the power of the individual, multiplied by the many:
Our world has changed. And needs to continue to change, with so much more left to do:

The terror. The horror. The pain. The change. In-process: even as we speak.

Graymoor – Croton – Hawthorne, NY
October 2001

(150) Hangin' Out on the Mountaintop: A Retreat Poem

for the Paramus Men's Group

Forty of us, *"the chosen of the chosen of the chosen,"*
Chose to climb this mountain. To spend the weekend, doing this work.

And Charley, looking like the old junkie, was there to lead us,
With the black FDNY cap turned backwards. And stories of seashells, and the face of G-d.

And most of the faces were familiar, but some of us were new,
As we gathered, again: the Friday night circle. This new beginning: again.

And it happens for each of us as it happens for each of us,
This sharing of fears; of tears; of successes. Where we are, today: the progress of our lives.

And the closing service began with Amazing Grace, and ended with America the Beautiful,
As each embraced each other: the blessings of fellowship; the grace of peace.

And down the mountaintop, back into the world, back into our lives;
Cruising at 75 on 287, foliage just past its peak: the bareness, beginning.

And the thruway. The Tappan Zee. And errands. And laundry. And home.
The experience; the teaching. To live fully: the curses. The blessings. Daily: All of it.

To rejoice. In where we are now. In who we are now   Here. Now. Today.

NJ — NY
October — November 2001

150.

FOR THOSE

WHO REMAIN

For Steve,

the Phelps Hospice Staff,

and the Volunteers

Author's Note

I saw a flyer offering training as a volunteer at Phelps Hospice at a church in Ossining in the spring of 1999. I had read a little of Elizabeth Kubler-Ross and Stephen Levine and Ram Dass on dealing with people in the final stages of life; it's an interest of mine; it's a state/place that will affect all of us. I wanted to learn more about this process, maybe become a bit more conscious of how to behave when the end approaches—and I expected that I'd meet some interesting people. I contacted Steve Bayer, the volunteer coordinator, went through six Monday evenings of training, and became a hospice volunteer. My experience in going through that time was addressed in the poem, "Hospice—the Training."

I've described the usual patient visit, for me, as essentially a "babysitting gig;" typically my role has been to visit the patient, and to be present in that room, and to allow the primary caretaker—usually the wife, the husband, or an adult child—a couple of hours to take care of other business, such as church, or meetings with social or support groups, etc. The patient is sometimes alert and aware of me, and may want to talk, or visit; other times they may be asleep throughout my time with them. Although my experience may not be typical, I've been told that people are coming into hospice at later stages; it's rare, therefore, that I get to see a patient more than once or twice. I'll usually get a phone call from Steve not long after my visit telling me that the patient has passed. It never comes as a surprise, of course, given these circumstances; but there's always that moment. Accepting that finality—that this phase, (at least, if one chooses to believe) is over.

I had an ulterior motive, I'll admit, in choosing this service. As a writer, I realize that there's more risk, more of a challenge—there's more at stake—when one tackles the larger issues. Death, and dying, and the quality of life at the end of life—these are large issues, core issues; these are, of course, very basic, human concerns. I put myself out to be of service in small ways, on a one-to-one basis; and if I listened well, if I paid attention, there's been much that can be learned from this work. Some of the poems in this book were written before I joined hospice; but all my work from this point on will be colored, in some way, by the experiences I've had—and continue to have—as a hospice volunteer.

Acceptance.
Remembrance.
Continuation.

Croton - Hawthorne, NY
1 October 2003

155.

(157) Watching Death's Labors

As if fallen from a tree before me
Was the irreparable

Though appearances deceive
The lady can afford to wait, this life is already hers

The seeming rescue, as an ornament to the work
The drainer of life begins with moisture: desiccation.

Dead browns and grays replace the magnesium green
The body shivers, contracts, withdraws into itself

The heavy, cellulosic stem, almost the last left alive
The tiny yellow seeds, the promise of resurrection

And though the dark lady shall own all that is material,
Mind and heart, spirit, idea: all beyond her cold, dead grasp.

NYC - NJ
May 88

(158) Poem: for My Father

I get a call from one or both your daughters,
Reminding me that it's one of the four times in the year;
Your only son does his duty, remembers, chant and spirit,
Intones your names, English and twisted Yiddish-Hebrew, in remembrance:
        the Maker of us all.

All my importances, so much you'd hate, only the surfaces you'd see, know and love,
Master of avoidance, becoming silent, turning away, discorporating your only son
Crushed by rejection, all your life I knew I was wrong,
Only now can I trust the limits of your love, trust my own needs, my growth:
        strange similitudes, father and son.

It's the beach at Rockaway, chilly, deserted, walking the shore,
Returning to boardwalk's safety, not surprised to meet your ghost, serene, strong,
Fifty-three-year-old form, wide man, dark topcoat, jaunty green felt fedora;
Dream, tasting oddly of life. I, who have no son, must do both our work:
        I carry you with me, always. I'm Alex's only son.

NYC
May—August 94

(159) Elegy
for Greg

No more the ordinary things, pushing blue buttons at the cash machine,
No more the scamming, the getting over, the so-smooth manipulations,
No more the charm, the big grin, the easy elegance, the well-dressed front:
No more the almost-hidden tears, the real & imagined sufferings: the little-boy pill-head.

In hospital, with neck brace laughing, healing, seemingly hopeful,
At PAX, with three days back, again, again,
Walking, after a meeting, talking literature: Kerouac, Bukowski, the St. Francis prayer;
Silent now, unsmiling. Maybe even with the pain of life lifted. Maybe.

The fourth name in my PAX phonebook crossed by the unforgiving shadow.
No more calls, no more running into on the street,
No more that brilliant, light-filled smile;
Maybe now he'll rest. Dropping the form we knew, with work left over for the next.

NYC - Rahway, NJ
September - October 96

(160) Hospice: The Training
for Steve & the volunteers

We won't know, we can't know
What's going on behind that door
The training does ground us, it gives a little information,
So we'll knock, and offer our help. In any way we can.

We've been told that we'll be dealing with patients, with their families;
What we will do is meet new people. At this crucial, critical, complicated time.
We'll show up, we'll offer our time, our selves, we'll speak little, listen more;
Fluid as water, moving to their direction, addressing their needs. *"It's not about us."*

Twenty self-selected strangers, six Monday evenings, one dropout:
The rest, ready to serve. At a service we can't begin to understand.
Now at the end of this beginning; the real work awaits.   Bringing open hearts,
Calm centers, the willingness to be fully human; we're ready as we can be.

An opportunity to be useful, to give support, perhaps to ease a little of the inevitable pain;
We become volunteers, eyes; ears; voices. For those who pass; for those who remain.

Croton - Montrose, NY
April 99

160.

(161) Poem: for Mrs. N.

Her drawn, wrinkled face, her curiosity, her energy,
Even at the end. Meeting without shared history,
The connection brief, but real. The few hours of an afternoon, an evening,
Learning from her at this, her time. An example: Grace. Warmth. Well-lived dignity.

She wanted to talk, to listen, to share,
Even smiled at the poetry, suggested, when I'd run out of things to say.
As Barbara walked in, I'd read the old Holiday poem, the end, the beginning:
"The gift is the circle…" She took my hand, in farewell. Five days later, the circle completed.

We do this because we choose to, because we think we can, because it helps, because of this:
To serve quietly, as this phase ends. To be strengthened, challenged; to be bettered by this service.

Montrose - Hawthorne, NY
February - March 01

(162) The Hand of God
for Bob

"The universe was not made in jest but in solemn
incomprehensible earnest, by a power that's
unfathomably secret, and holy, and fleet."
—Annie Dillard, Pilgrim at Tinker Creek

A book of amazing images: the Hubble space-based telescope
Star systems, nebulae, and galaxies, even of hidden black holes,
Some so distant, others *"near neighbors…only 40 million light years away"*
A sense of wonder, of immense Power; and of arrogance of mind, claiming connection to it all.

But I am that living spark of consciousness, call it chi, light, life, spirit, soul,
That which quickens me, that ineffable beyond mere matter, beyond all chemistries,
I know it lives in me, in all; it comforts, to think, *"there, there's the connection"*:
To the One who knows equally: the falling of the sparrow. The birth of the star.

Whitman's quoted, walking out on *"the learn'd astronomer,"*
To walk *"the mystical moist night air,"* to gaze *"in perfect silence at the stars."*
I'm glad of the science, our many vast learnings, theories tried, tested, toppled;
But science can't break the limits of itself. Science explains; faith remains.

Images of vastness, of violence, in true color and false:
My breath, my heart, my soul, my silence, my truth, my faith:

I remain connected.

Ossining - Croton, NY
May 02

Note: Written after reading **The Hand of God**, ed. Michael Reagan
(Lionheart Books, Atlanta, GA, 1999).

162.

(163) The Genesis of Hope
for Robyn

"How wrong Emily Dickinson was! Hope is not 'the thing with
feathers.' The thing with feathers has turned out to be my
nephew. I must take him to a specialist in Zurich."
—*Woody Allen*

New York City: The Center for a Science of Hope.
Interfacing biology, theology, genetics, philosophy,
Positing the premise, the possibility: that hope resides within the stuff of our genes;
That emotions *are* borne of electrochemistry; to be measured, understood; perhaps even changed

And if hope, or fear, or joy, or ease, may yet be quantified,
Perhaps the soul itself might yet be observed: weighed; analyzed; visualized
By spectrophotometers yet-to-be conceived, chromatography past Kirlian, undreamed-of, today;
But not impossible. This new land, this interface, science and spirit: open, to the new pioneers.

The Seattle office worker hoping a break in the clouds
The generations of Jews hoping the rebuilding, the Messiah
The terminal patient hoping the turning away, the fast-spreading cancer
The love-starved imagining his special one: that hope, that *sine qua non*, of our very beings.

And what of the hopeless, the addict, the burned, the lost, the terrified—
Lives can be transformed, tiny miracles do happen, we've seen 'em all so often on our tv's.
So perhaps it's the *potential* for hope that's built-into the system; perhaps the Grand Designer
Left the door open. For us to choose our own heaven, or hell—our own darkness, or light.

I want the science, I know it, I trust it, but believe it not limitless;
This scale too vast to be conquered, in my small years.
But dialogue, learning, faith; all may co-exist, smilingly,
Physicists, philosophers, all asking the same questions:

And each of those more important than any answer.

Hawthorne - Croton, NY/May - June 2002

(164) "He Picked People Up"
for Rocco

One of the principles we're told to practice is acceptance,
That some things can be changed while some others—cannot.
We want—I want—to believe that there's meaning, purpose, beyond my shortsighted view;
So I can't rail, at the injustice. For the real understanding, the bigger picture's—just not mine, to know.

At the small step meeting, he'd be the first to volunteer—engineer boots, cowboy hat, and opinions,
The last of which he had no problem in sharing. Talkin' fourth step, talkin' retreat:
"If they've got a name for it, pally, someone else's done it."
He liked to talk—co-founded *"On'an'on"*—but mostly it was because he had something to say.

"Daddy's Bible" in the box with him, though it wasn't him in the box,
Just the shell, the limits of flesh. The closed eyes, the limp fingers; the black suit.
Brother Dennis taught him: if the faith is true the wine **becomes** the holy blood,
And even an alcoholic can't get drunk on the blood of the lamb.

At seventeen, he knew he'd go to hell. At thirty-nine, I know he hasn't.
He's pulled up his tent; he's finished his traveling. Finally—he's come home.

Hartsdale, NY – Wharton, NJ
September 2002

KYZEN:

SELECTED POEMS

Illustrated by Ryn Gargulinski

For Bill Wilson and Bob Smith

and

For Ryn

(169) Kyzen[1]: What It's About

Been writing these things more than 30 years, the changes:
External, internal, subtle, gross; apartments, jobs,
The various men and women in & out my life:
Reflected, this self-history; this continuing work.

For this new project, I'd pulled out old stained typewritten pages,
Read through poems no one's ever seen, others
I hadn't looked at in fifteen years, and more;
Selected these, from those. Twice *chai* [2] poems, '74 - 2004.

Not a great career, not widely known, certainly not done for the bucks,
But this note's written while flying from Paris to Newark, and the headphones
Give the gift, the great Ella, sweetly, *"Lullaby of Birdland."* **Art lives**, and for me,
It's not music, film, painting; poetry's my only art. It's what's been given to me.

It's in your hands now, listen or accept or laugh or judge: it's what I've done, it's what I do;
Kyzen: perpetual improvement. The process, the journey; the here, the now; always: today.

> Paris - Newark; Croton - Montreal; Croton, NY
> October - December 04

[1]*Kyzen*: Japanese for "continuous or perpetual improvement."
[2]*chai*: Yiddish for "life," or the number 18; there are 36 poems in the (original) collection
        (in addition to this introduction).

(171) Beat Youth

It's the darkness, man, the
Darkness
     that laughs with the evil of the vamp.

It's the wildness, man, the
Wildness
     that greets the gray of dawn.

It's the lifelove, man, the
Lifelove
     that lives the energy of youth.

It is the celebration of magnificence
It is the power of possibility
It is the smile that is rejected
     that teaches
     that continues to smile.

Now alone in the universe
Universeye grinning brightly
     An ash falls on the sand of a holiday beach
     Impermanent as youth

Rockaway Beach, NY
July 74

171.

(172) Saturday Afternoon 2/7/76

I've been in a pissed-off state for several days,
I see the dept. screwing me, right, left, upside down & royally
The grades, the lab, the money
                    the G-d-damned money.
But I'm praying a lot more, I'm writing some,
There are good times to be had with friends, like last night,
The movie, the company, the smoke
I even read two poems to them,
Bukowski and Bukowski and Bukowski
And now I'm still reading Bukowski

(But as I type the ribbon dries up
like so many lives that I've known)
There is music as I typewrite. I watch the guts of this inked image transformer.
Burning in Water, Drowning in Flame.
Orange cover, 228 pages, bought in Pittsburgh a year ago,
Poems, poems, more:
            so I stop my words & listen to some better ones.

If you're pissed off, hear Buk on the bosses:
> *"the bosses, yellow men with bad breath and big feet, men who look like frogs,
> hyenas, men who walk as if melody had never been invented, men...who'd kill
> you because they're crazy and justify it because it's the law, men who stand in
> front of windows 30 feet wide and see nothing,,,men like snails, men like eels,
> men like slugs, and not as good..."*[1]

Thanks, Buk.
            Here at Tulane
            Some people study poetry
            But not too many read it.

1. Charles Bukowski, *Burning in Water, Drowning in Flame: Selected Poems 1955 – 1973*
    (HarperCollins, 1974)

New Orleans/February 76

172.

(173) "How a Friendship Emerges"

The process: scaling human walls.
Initial caution. Fears. Distrust. Histories.
Time. The growth of caring, understanding. Time.
The rose of two hearts, two beings enriched.

NYC
July 87

Poem for Mary (A Florida Poem)

The dark spirits of Water and Air obscured my southern days.

She was blonde, her pure white smiles my beacon, yet
I knew I lacked her needs. I swam upstream, for show or for love—?

I cry the gentler Spirits to caress her, to deliver to her:
Her One. The one who is not me.

West Palm Beach, FL - Newark, NJ
November 87

173.

(174) what can we learn from Coyote

(175) Chant

"...that we are many selves looking at
each other, through the same eye."
--Gary Snyder, **The Old Ways**

What can we learn from our readings
What can we learn from our vision
What can we learn from our noble ones
What can we learn from our savages

What can we learn from our CD's
What can we learn from Al Roker
What can we learn from the darkness approaching
What can we learn from the new autumn light

What can we learn from our prosecutors
What can we learn from our panhandlers
What can we learn from our union leaders
What can we learn from our homeboys

What can we learn from our quiet oceans
What can we learn from our mountains into ski trails
What can we learn from our child-beaters
What can we learn from our NAMBLAs

What can we learn from our skydivers
What can we learn from our porn stars
What can we learn from our Jesse Helmses
What can we learn from our Karen Finleys

What can we learn from our speed-freaks
What can we learn from our crack-heads
What can we learn from our Gordon Liddys
What can we learn from our Timothy Learys

What can we learn from our Bhagavans
What can we learn from our O'Connors
What can we learn from our Black Elks
What can we learn from our Ram Dass

What can we learn from our Bear
What can we learn from our Snake
What can we learn from our Eagle
What can we learn from our Coyote

What can we learn
What can we learn
What can we learn
What can we learn

**"All that is in this sphere
All that is in all spheres
All may be known. There are no limits."**

NYC
September 90

(177) KK's: Breakfast

The Saturday warm for December; pseudo-scientists blaming the misunderstood Greenhouse,
Others simply accepting the bright clear autumn.
Woke of a Saturday with dulling errands before me,
Allowing for the treat, the once-the-norm: KK's. Breakfast.

Much more crowded than expected, late, almost one,
Through the small smoking section, lucking out, table for two by the pole near the back.
Tables filled with animated laughter, intense eyes ingesting partner's words,
Another treat: blintzes, cheese and apple. Juice. The necessary coffee.

I remember bringing her here Sunday mornings, after dark sweet nights together,
Noting my sullenness over pancakes, knowing the pain that I didn't need her;
Knowing that someday, I'd have to tell her. Hiding my truth in sweet tan coffees,
In the movement of First Avenue: the large clean window.

Escaping work a warm spring day, lingering here over coffees, I wrote of madness,
                of choices, of the desperate living need for hope
A Tuesday night, the room deserted; I gobbled my pierogi. It was enough.
Sweet apple and cheese, smooth sour cream in my mouth; breakfast, Saturday,
                more errands yet to do;
In the warm, soft light, in the comfort of half-a-hundred voices; a meal; a haven:
        KK's: New York City.

NYC
December 90

177.

(178) Toward A Poetry With Balls

To include Sinatra, Joplin, Berlin, Yo-Yo Ma,
Calder, Gauguin, Hopper, Van Gogh,
Oppenheimer, Feynman, Carrothers, Gould,
Sandberg, Cummings, Ginsberg and Whitman:

To include hot salsa, hot asphalt, hot NYC summer,
Silent beach, hyper sandpipers, miserably perfect February,
Vegetative death, crunch of brown leaves, return of old darkness,
Holy new energy, green new birth, the annual gift: to begin, again;

To include the laughter of the tickled newborn, the virginal glow of the satisfied bride,
The junkie's shaky spasm, midnight spasms of hot mutual climax,
Lead pipe breaking jawbone, blade seeking its living sheath,
The comforting phone call, inevitable acceptance: the power to change;

Not the moon and the stars, but the breath of life: creation;
Guiltless, unashamed, singing, being—as we are. As we can become.

NYC - NJ
August -September 90

178.

(179) toward a poetry with balls

179.

(180) *For the Wedding of Angelo and Katherine*

Recent studies have shown
(Though still subject to much controversy)
That the only other species on this planet
Capable of that miracle beyond understanding
(I refer, of course, to that singular wonder,
That blindingly complex phenomenon known colloquially as *love*)
Is…the butterfly.

There's even one report
That on warm spring evenings
When the pre-metamorphosized young
are safely, quietly asleep
The two in love watch videos of sunsets and dark seas,
Hear primordial sounds known by their cells, if not yet by their minds,
Cuddle warmly as only two in love might;

Further studies are indicated.

NYC - NJ
April 93

(181) butterfly

181.

(182) Belated Poem: for Mary

I wanted to write words that would change your life,
Words to force your radiance onto your disbelief,
Wanted to strip away cold sorrow, give you the glorious angel you truly are

Words are floating feathered seeds on dark silent beaches,
Drops of sweet honey on the graying, drying mud,
The last breathing candle; the generous, overwhelming night

This arrives late, but you understand,
The sadnesses of time; the natural, logical separations.
The rarity of connections; truly, as it's supposed to be.

But, given our limits, our special magic's still new, still re-creating,
Phone calls and imaginings, desires only for the other's good;
Our embrace remains strong, this healthy love is real;
      our separate lives, together, continue.

NYC
May 93

(183) Poem: for the Woman with the Scar on Her Neck

Healing is a gift, an art, an energy; it is rebirth, renewal, the promise of new life;

Technology has power, but the invisible gives more,

You who are changing, becoming, entering new health, new life, new being:

Live love, with your partner. The noblest force shall make you whole.

NYC
March 95

Letter to Myself

Anger better than wimp depression
Understanding better than brutal anger
Self-forgiving better than understanding
Self-forgetting better than self-forgiving

Self-forgetting leading to Positive Action
Positive Action leading to New Situations.

Oxford Valley, PA – Hawthorne, NY
August 97 – April 99

(184) turtle rising to the ring

(185) For the Retreatants

The pain of the loss of the many-just-met,

The illusion of loss, of pain;

The songs of the birds,

The rain; the sun.

Omega, Rhinebeck, NY
July 93

"For Ram Dass, My Great Teacher: In Recovery"

*"It's not the sea breeze, the blue-white-gray of the April sky,
not the urban asphalt-and-concrete, the yellowness
of the taxicabs, the quiet of the closed bar across
the street; it's not.*

*"It's the fullness in every breath, in every thought,
in the billions of impulses that move us all;*

*"It is the turtle rising to the ring. It is our gift, our joy,
our suffering; it is what we are given."*

Namaste.

NYC - NJ
April 97

185.

(186) Poem: for Joanie

Secrets are burdensome things, weighty beings hiding in protective lies
But we've learned their horror's imaginary, their power's only as dust

Wanting now, to tell you,
Somewhere, quietly, within

Image of man loving woman, alone, the sauna, just after lunch
Her lead, his desired follow, warm damp bodies, man's mouth and tongue,
      woman's hot furry center, the unquiet turn-around of maybe--
      getting caught--and--and--
      so what if we were caught...!

Too brief, so damned brief
But a loving truth remains

A glorious moment
Frozen, behind my eyes

NYC
August - September 93

186.

(187) Pax – II

for Bob, Charlie, Roy, Robert, et al.

The men that gather here, in this room
Spend chilly hours breathing dark winter tales,
Sweat thick summer hours accepting knowledge, power, life;
Keep returning, the white-enameled basement. The quiet, well-lit center.

That man walked out nine drunken car wrecks, nine blessings given,
Broke his spine on the tenth; now he laughs and teaches from his chair.
Those two guys are beating cancer. The guy with HIV's run three marathons.
Here we talk of fear. Here we conquer much of it.

We choose this process, bitch and burn at its slowness, its damned immensity,
Scream our wrong moves, risks lost and won, amazing new learnings;
Each new moment brings the brilliance of hope, of growth, of humanity:
The process changes each man. The gentle light increases, invisibly, within.

Sixty men laughing, listening, this same simple church basement;
"How" is the wrong question. The only answer is: *yes.*

NYC
October 93

(188) "...I Can't Go to Astoria Without Thinking of Her."

I didn't cruise by the apartment. I did in the past
Saw Halloween cardboards in what had been her window; drove on.
Eight years gone now, ten tiny weeks together, her hot winter bed.
My rigorous truth, her natural terror; the talking, the testing meant nothing;
The relationship, of course, had to end--with much, much pain.

When I stopped visiting, the living spirit of her hatred remained,
Knife-like glares, twisted mouth, fair skin hot, blotchy, body tight, coiled;
Obsessively, my unquiet mind, her vengeful need; shared belief, deserved guilt,
Wishing for pain's removal, her haunting genuine, near-constant:
The torment somehow, horribly, serving me.

I remember the woman who'd loved me, remember the same, hideously embittered,
Knowing always I'd done wrong, yet knowing I'd done all I could to correct.
Amends never enough, never could be. Finally accepting, for today: they must be.
Putting her image behind, no longer willing to carry her cross:
The out-breath of a freedom, finally claimed.

Saturday night open, heard two fine poets at the Broadway reading;
Astoria. Still hers, I imagine. My wrongs unforgiven, save by me;
      The thread is broken. Quiet, now...perhaps the past can finally rest.

NYC
November 93 - January 94

188.

(189) In My Mailbox Today: A Found Poem

Arlo Guthrie's Rolling Blunder Review Concert in Stamford, CT, March 24

Toxikon Corporation "Received res, we'll let'cha know"

St. John's University Alumni placement newsletter

State of New Jersey, Dept.of Labor Unemployment check

Mary Leary *"Got any poems, Phil?"*

Calgene Chemical Corporation *"We regret to inform you that..."*

Beth Israel Medical Center Health Line—Information

Publisher Inquiry Services *"America's Most Wanted Catalogs"*

Fantasy, Inc. Music Catalog

Precision Cleaning Magazine Invitation to show, Chicago, May

Omega Institute for Holistic Studies *"The Path to Discovery"* catalog

NYC
March 95

189.

(190) NYC - Morrisville

This is about change, about rebirth, balance, strength, even financial success;
No. It's about relief from pain, elimination of true unhappiness, the need for the deep quiet breath.
The desire for All, for mind, heart, sex, soul, money, work,
Caused this great movement. To leave the turbulent Center; to drive away from Oz.

The new apartment is large, warm, carpeted. I hang my Magrittes, my Melovas, my Papens,
Store my too-many books, my too-many conflicting papers, the black box gives me
Basie & Blues Brothers on albums, John Lennon on CD;
The large, solitary apartment, a living thing: slowly, becoming my home.

Two weeks at work, amazingly, my opinion sought, respected;
 (I still know little, but history serves me well, here.)
Still deeply in the self-dug hole of dollars, still sleep alone, without desired, loving warmth,
All just baggage, karma of this life. I begin again: carrying my past, smiling, welcoming my future.

This is about change, but more, it's about continuation:
For my friends, for all who've touched my heart: remember. Stay with me, as I, with you. In love.

NYC - NJ - PA
August 97

190.

(191) Valentine's Day
for Beth

The blanket on the carpeted floor, sandalwood incense, warm candles,
Quiet samba, guitar & tenor. You lie back, stilly fully clothed,
Eyes half-mast; expectant; waiting. "Relax," I croon,
For this is sacred pleasure: this is our time, together.

Hovering over you, taking in your shape, your form,
Loving you with my eyes, even before touch, before tongue.
Our lips meeting gently, passion almost-controlled,
The kiss deepens, tongues flare, hands rise to bare belly, to satin bra'd breasts;
The so-sweet, so-sensitive nipples. And your gasps—and I thrill to the sounds.

My hands now on your belly and thighs, quickly your clothes fall, as
Quickly do mine, two now-naked lovers, lips tightly pressed,
Belly to hot belly, hotly pressing bellies, too quick, slow down my love slow--!
We pull apart, and again, desire!, fingers, lips, your life-giving breasts!
Though I fear giving pain, your sharp moaning inbreaths: joys, unknown, to me.

My hands between your legs, sacred woman-moisture beginning,
I guide your head between my legs, for your pleasures, for mine.
Reversing, this my need, tongue hard against magic hidden button,
        my fingers aswim, your thickening honey,
And here: your deep pleasures, unknown to me. And here: mine, to you.
As a gift, a dessert: you astride me, me deep in you. And your sweet moanings.

These brief moments, body to body: histories, codependence ignored:
Warm, the music, the blanket, the carpeted floor. Lovingly cuddling:
        sharing, this special, love-filled pleasure.

Morrisville PA -- Hamilton NJ
February 98

191.

(192) Morrisville to Croton

*"Hey, didn't he write the same
kind of poem last year?"*

It's too early for this poem. Books in boxes still litter the living room,
Cheap steel shelving slowly rising, the wall of words today only a dream,
Thousands of pages in brown kraft, kraft in corrugated, corrugated in closets, access a distant dream;
I've moved, again. A one-bedroom, in Westchester. The apartment. The new job. Again. Again.

If one accepts *"manageability "* as illusion, I'm doing just fine, thanks.
Saturday morning brings errands, bankcard in search of new PIN number,
Withdrawal, Post Office, tailor, pharmacy, salami & swiss at diner:
What remains: develop the apartment. And the inner work: even on this glorious day.

Fear-filled for a month or more, the good news of new job giving powerful change,
Change: and its dreadful complications. But it appears I've survived thus far,
Emotionally, physically, spiritually—amazingly, even financially,
And calm patient steps on this new given path may yet give new, real growth.

The calendar reads early autumn, but the fountain'd duck pond seems summer;
These the days of awe, this again the true time, again the true turning of the year.
We begin again. Job-feeling's hopeful, apartment's becoming, meetings are welcoming, HP still lives:
"What a long, strange trip it's been." It helps if I give up control.

Still connected to my history, East Village to LA, Tucson & NOLA to Morrisville, but here; now.
My third coffee, breakfast at the diner, Croton-on-Hudson, New York: I am. I remain. I am.

Croton-on-Hudson, NY
September 98

192.

(193) Poem: for My Bathroom Wall

It's a measure of my sexual isolation, I've been told, I know it's true,
Such vast ranges of fantasy. But attraction's so sweet, lusts run so high,
At these simple paper cutouts, these triggers of oceans of sexual joys--
Glorious women, fantastic men! And not either/or, but Yes. Yes. Yes.

The crew-cutted Asian boy, the public strut, corset, stockings, big liberated grin of freedom,
The gun-toting topless sisters, Black, Brown, & Beige;
Her warmly welcoming thighs, the tiny orange thong bikini,
His buff blond come-on smirk, her gentle eyes--this electrifying landscape,
                this hot tight lusty forest!

My bed's shared by few, sex with mind predominates,
Not unsatisfying--still, it's alone. Pantomimes with unseen voices, well-worn photos & text,
Human connection failing me, not forever, but for now. Still, this shining spirit enlivens me:
A healthy, holy, living sexuality--a blessing, in the learning.

The great desire: for wisdom in this work, this sweet gift, this pleasure-play;
To learn its proper use, this karmic connection. The strangeness of my higher path.

Ossining – Croton – Hawthorne, NY
February – April 99

193.

(194) heap o'dead bodies

194.

(195) Level 3 Poem
for Stan

They lined us up, naked, on the floor
Silent rows of what might be firewood
Still alive at that moment, we could hear the directions
Preparing ourselves. For the darkness-yet-to-come.

On my deathbed, an hour, maybe two, the inevitable end,
A small darkened bedroom, a curtain, a second room filled with life,
My tall Uncle Sam, my sisters, even lovers I thought'd left me behind;
The crowded outer room. While I lay dying, alone.

Alone, as I'd lived, superficial, fear-filled, terrified of all you people,
Wanting, yet protecting; always pushing the world away.
Feel the self-pity, the loneliness, the screaming silent sadness, my empty heart:
And it took years for the dying man to learn: **TEAR DOWN THE CURTAIN!**

The love-as-people flooded the room, I weep with their caresses;
It is my time; yes, I die. But know: the love which was given to me, this life:

And know: the love I may yet give. This life.

Princeton - Trenton, NJ
July 98

195.

(196) Continuity
for Gina

Autumn. The smooth surface of the lake,
Red-bodied dragonfly, yellow working bumblebee;
Crossing to the far shore, the spiral of the sad leaf, the light summery breeze:
You, leaving for the West. For the good.

The many gifts before me, the brightly-colored landscape,
The pale blue daisies, the second coming of butter-and-egg,
The rocky earth beneath my feet, the clearly marked path I do follow—
A decade, our true, unique connection; a difficult, sober, rarely-seen love.

Nothing's new here, simply Change's continuity, the transparency of the appearance of endings,
Neither sweet, nor bitter (unless I choose to make it so).
All that you've given to me, all you've meant to me: immeasurable, in the silence:
The light of the moon trapped in a Mason jar. The warmth of two heartbeats, shared; become one.

The trail winds, yellow leaves floating, the green shallows, the end of the lake;
As an old couple walking, as initials carved on a tree: as symbol, as breath, as personal choice:
    All that is good in me, remains, with you. Today. Always.

Rockefeller State Park, North Tarrytown, NY
October 99

(197) On the Pleasures of Empty Sex
for Billy, Tom, Harry, et al.

Too many years in the dim lights of steam and sauna,
Not yet left behind, but know it now, a sad, dead end.
Desire-dance with shadowed strangers, illusions of intimacy,
Still, these darkened rooms served me. The needs of the body;
            the limitations of the baths.

Phone lines and personals, occasional meetings,
Blind dates at Borders; propositions, rejections, acceptances;
To his place, to my place, or not (two yesses required);
Two strangers, deep embrace. A level above; some minor progress.

Meeting a man at the workshop, eye contact, touch, energy rising,
Two weeks later in his bed, youth to his man, sharing the fuck.
The phones again, my hometown, ten minutes, another man's bed;
Two strangers kissing, kissing; kissing 'til we come.

The steps on this path, lonely guilt to meeting new men,
The joys of flesh; beginnings, connections, intimacies, lovers.

Toward self-acceptance; toward self-love:
To live that love; to share it; to give my love away.

Convent Station, NJ
May 2000

197.

(198) On Reading The Sunday Times Magazine at Pete's, Sunday, 3/18/01
(A Found Poem: Approximately)

The depth and wealth and richness of our culture

From Safire's treatise on Having It All
To photojournalism: after the school shooting

From the new movie based on the Hemingway story
To the *"brutal and beautiful"* new Mexican film

From art forgeries to *"No Justice No Peace"*
From American morality to Land's End swimsuits

From cool blue furniture ads and smiling Amerasian models
To rack of lamb and luxury estates

From camps, schools and shopping at home
To an Eileen Fisher ad that looks like the Colors of Benneton hit middle age

82 glossy pages, counting the Salvatore Ferragamo fold-out cover
 While the business section's Data Bank states that the *"Bear Market Becomes a Reality"*

Noted, for the record, at Pete's, on Atlantic, 3/18/01
Two weeks before they'll be forced by the landlord to close up shop

A Lemon Zinger tea, a butter pecan cookie, a chocolate chip cookie;
A Sunday, writing alone. Pete's. Just before leaving Brooklyn.

Brooklyn - Croton, NY
March 2001

198.

(199) On Tennessee: Cry of the Heart

for Dotson

The hard-covered book was only a dollar; the bookstand, Montague Street,
I'd walked to the center of the Heights after the reading, buying Catullus and Troy Perry,
And Rader. And Williams. Nursing a large coffee at the trendy coffee bar:
"And all it all cost was ten dollars and I felt like a rich man."

Took my time with the book. Wanted to savor it, the life & times, my NYC, the 70's;
Starting in the 60's I'd discovered second-hand bookstores—now gone, all gone! —
Evergreen Reviews. Read Rader, on radicalism; on sex. Young. Scared. Closeted.
Self-hating, short & fat & lonely. And gay. And I drank and I smoked. To hide. To hide.

And Tennessee was our greatest living playwright. I saw him on stage, as Doc,
"Small Craft Warnings," with Candy Darling, a little theater, the east 50's, maybe.
Saw him lying at Campbell's Funeral Home, an empty room; Dakin, in a black suit;
I mumbled a few words to the brother; he seemed distracted, confused.

The 70's, saw Yevtushenko at the Felt Forum, perhaps the same performance that they saw,
Saddened, the Commissar at the Oak Room, the Plaza Hotel, enjoying the spoils of capitalism;
Saddened, the reality: ego, intolerance. From the man who wrote, *"The Spirit of Elbe."*
But I remember that evening, so important for me, so very long ago:

After the reading, feeling strong, adult, I took the subway back home to Rockaway,
A Friday night, my father drinking with his friend, Joe the Butcher, Joe the *Shika*;
I helped myself to his Canadian Club, first time I'd dared drink in front of my father,
Wanting to drink with him. Wanting his approval, wanting his love.

The very young wannabe poet, still a boy, in the house of his father:
My silent father stayed silent. I felt the sad disapproval in his eyes;
I drank; he didn't. I kept drinking, talked of the Russian poet I'd seen that night:
I never drank with my father. It was always his choice; it was always his house.

    "No one gets outa this life alive…"

(200) On Tennessee: Cry of the Heart (cont.)

A hardbound book on the grass of Charles Point, Peekskill, New York;
Sunning myself; the hottest day of the year. The great dust jacket photo,
The smaller, goateed writer, embraced by his taller, loving friend;
The generous, giving, empty sea; the Great Mother, behind.

> *It's still important*
> *To read*
> *To write*
> *To listen*
> *To remember:*

Tennessee Williams. 1911 - 1983.

Peekskill - Croton, NY
June - July 2001

(201) My Gorka Connection
for Andrea

Just after Christmas, we came into Bethlehem;
Bethlehem, PA. She'd booked us into a bed-and-breakfast
(But I always think of Judy when I think bed-and-breakfast, turning her 79th St. apartment into one)
But that was years before we'd met

We'd met one Sunday in a hotel meeting room, midtown,
Where Chip led thirty or so of us in a one-day introduction to intimacy.
A couple of weeks later I called. We had dinner at a Chinese restaurant, Madison, New Jersey,
Where two stone dragon-dogs guarded the door.

We saw *"The English Patient"*—a woman's movie—but I liked it more than she did.
Saw Li-Young Lee and Billy Collins and Ginsberg intoning *"Hum Bom"* under the big tent at Waterloo.
She had the Ph.D. I never got, I always figured she made more money than I did
But she only wrote poems to sing her depression. The poems weren't bad; weren't happy, either.

Once before sleep, we created our own ritual, honoring each other's chakras,
With oil and blessings and kisses, first one, then the other, from the base to the crown.
We'd tried it a second time and for some reason it didn't work as well—
But our loving was sweet and satisfying. Though it lasted less than six months.

Our time was driven by that lovemaking,
The energy ran out after the first of the year.
But it was First Night in Oakland, with Lucy Kaplansky and Richard Shindell,
And John Gorka in a little club in Bethlehem, just after Christmas. Five years ago.

Now it's the muddy crowd at Clearwater, just after the rain,
And it's Tom Rush, and John Gorka, with Dar Williams coming up.
She always needed *live* music, she showed and taught me so much:
Her household goddesses. Her dance. Her service. Her love.

The willow full in June, the golden thread of the Hudson, the Palisades smoky after the rain,
Dar Williams singing of Spring Street, of not fearing women, and *"Turn, Turn, Turn,"* with Pete.
We did touch, we did connect, albeit briefly; it did matter, does matter, does matter still:
The heavy rain, before the end of the set. Soaking, sadly, the rain, the mud: Clearwater, 2002.

Croton – Hawthorne, NY
June 2002

201.

(202) *Tootsie's funeral*

(203) Because You Asked: A Belated Birthday Poem

for Ryn

Memorial Day: the quiet of northwest New Jersey
A flag in the breeze, the rich green lawn, the songs of the birds
Two-foot-tall Christmas trees, a Christmas tree farm, across the road
It took what it took to get to here:

Yesterday, Westchester, up & out early on a Sunday morning,
The black Toyota, 9A, the Saw Mill, 87, Triboro, GCP, Jackie Robinson
To Salem Fields on the edge of asphalt and concrete Jamaica Avenue,
A field now crowded with graying stones, and mausoleums

To be at the final service for Tootsie Silver, born six years after Kitty Hawk,
    who painted and drove ambulance in wartime and spent six weeks
    in a coma, the nursing home, Long Beach, just before the end

Psalms were read.
Clothing was (symbolically) torn.
The *Kaddish* was recited.
And Tootsie was laid to rest.

And the black Toyota took me onto Atlantic Avenue, over the Brooklyn Bridge into
    Whitman's Manhatta, onto Hudson Street north, through the Engineer's tunnel,
    over Pulaski's skyway, 78 deep into Jersey, 78 to 287 and still further west,
    finally, to the home by the high school, Hunterdon County,
    northwest New Jersey

To the house of a friend of a friend, for a shortened holiday weekend

And I think about you today, Memorial Day, your day; perhaps you're at a reading
    today, perhaps you're performing with 2/3 of The Nerve, perhaps you have
    plans, a quiet dinner, perhaps an evening with friends, perhaps you're writing

Somehow, I believe, along with everything else, you're writing, today.

Sometimes it's hard to find the space & time to write when the words want to flow

For a week I pushed, I tried too hard, wrote my introductory "*Whad'yawannasay*"
       at the tops of blank white index cards just under the words "*Ryn Poem: Notes*"

I close my eyes
Embrace the emptiness
Feel it lovingly embrace me

I bring the concept of "*Ryn's Birthday*" into the emptiness

The silence glows gold, silver, violet
Great pleasure, easy joy: the relaxed, glowing silence
Intimations of a Power so far beyond the pale limits of words

Tootsie's funeral: the past
The weekend, Jersey: the past
Your birthday: the past

The crest of the wave
The past, the future: *illusion*

But you remain shining in my mind
Brightly alive in the glowing violet silence

                     Hunterdon County, NJ - NYC - Croton, NY
                     May 2002

(205) Croton to the SCC: December 2002

Within the narrow space, the middle seat: Metro North,
Southbound into Grand Central, snow beginning, starting to stick,
Overslept by two hours, nothing to do now, just do;
The gray sky; the pale, gray-blue river. Morning; Thursday; December; snow.

Rick's recent gift, **Blonde on Blonde** CD, played repeatedly in the car last week
Thinking Dylan as popstar, Dylan as poet, Dylan just before he broke his neck.
Thinking ambition, *"success, power, toys"*—somehow, slowly, it all seems to be coming:
Gus' line last night: *"Beware the man who's proud of his own humility."* Noted. With caution.

This all seems to be about being of service, about living service, but it also seems,
Somehow, about getting what you want, or, even more, somehow, about getting what *I* want;
I know the work that's before me. Even now, other hands push colored pins into pressed
        cardboard, the bismuth oxychloride poster rises,
While I'm still in the middle seat: *Phylum Mollusca* studied at my left; virtual solitaire, the
        brightly-lit screen, the laptop, at my right.

The train rolls slowly, stops; snow's falling in earnest, now; just a day, just another
Working day; just the getting to the gig. And it's different, yeah,
But we've done this before. 125th Street. Manhattan. And we're almost there:
To stand in front of the poster, to extol the benefits of this pigment. To believe in what I say.
Snow, the streets; Rockefeller Center, the tree; NBC staff's yearly caroling, the skating rink, below:
New York City. The Meeting. The Poster. The Party, tonight. Maybe even the Hard Rock;

This: my work. Today.

Croton-on-Hudson, NY - NYC
December 2002

205.

(206) *Photograph: China Pier, January*
after David Whyte

I don't know the fish below the surface, this cold gray river

But I do know that icy-smooth, deceptively-moving surface,

Know that hill across, leafless trees blanketed with pure white

Know this light, the thick, slow-moving clouds, this still, winter air,

Know the bridge, now barely-visible, our hill meeting their hill,

Know the freshly-painted smokestack, pale gray column rising, still-paler clouds,

Know the grass, silently, dormantly alive, beneath the still white silence,

Know the few lone footprints

The ugly rusting statue

The wooden pier

The mountains

The river;

The river;

The river.

Peekskill - Croton, NY
January 2003

206.

(207) fish below the surface

(208) why I can't write...nobody cares

(209) Why I Can't Write

for The Famous Poet

It has to do with self-esteem, I'm told, or maybe even with self-love
And though I've worked on myself and I continue to work on myself ,
      sometimes I'm still low on that
But more it seems to be about why
Why bother why try; who cares, anyway
Who cares, indeed

And for a long time it didn't matter
It mattered to me and I could show them or read them or not but I felt that I knew what I was doing,
I knew what I was trying to do, I was trying to make the poem better and I knew it was a process
      and I knew I was connected, I knew I was part of that ongoing procession of poets, from
      Homer to Whitman to Ferlinghetti to Ginsberg to Lowell and Rich and Auden and Doty
      and Liu and Lorde and all of 'em—
I knew. I *knew* that I was one a'them. And it made me feel good. It made me feel connected.

And in March, I saw The Famous Poet at the reading, and he read well and he smiled and
      he chatted and he signed his books and he left before the open, so he didn't hear me,
      didn't hear the poem that I'd dedicated to hlm
And I featured twice in April, twice in Manhattan, and half-a-dozen people, or less, showed up
And nobody cares, the self-pitier cried, nobody cares, my deathless poems, my great work,
      this work I'd been born to do, this work that I'm doing, and I'm doing it so well,
      listen to me, hear me, and nobody's listening and nobody shows, and nobody cares,
      and even I stop caring

Stuck.
Stuck *exactly* there, for *months*, now:
Stuck big-time.

Wanting. Wanting that wealth and fame and power and adoration. The New York Times
      Book Review. The cash advance. The books on display at Barnes & Noble.
      So much. So much I'd wanted. Wanted. And so much I still want. Still want.

209.

(210) Why I Can't Write (cont).

And seeing The Famous Poet, who has all that. Wealth. Fame. Love. Or so it seemed.
    So it seems.

And he read at the reading and he smiled and he chatted and he signed his books
    and then he left. And I know that he's lucky if he's able to do that half-a-dozen
    times in a month, 'cause his gig is the professorship, the various universities
    ('cause we all need the day job);

BUT I ENVIED HIM. I ENVIED HIM SO MUCH.

Gay. Out. Successful! Successful as a writer—as a poet, even! Successful as a *poet*!
    In this culture! The Book Reviews. The cash advances. The books on display.
    The requests to speak at conferences. The audiences who pay to hear him:
ENVY. OWNING MY OWN ENVY.

And I'm no longer (chronologically) young. I can't be a younger poet, not at my age.
    When I read on the circuit I'll get my polite applause. The poems do occasionally
     land in the little magazines, but those by their very nature seem mostly unread.
    I compare myself to him and find myself wanting, wanting;
Stuck so deeply in that unlovely thing, my own envy. Greener than Shrek, uglier than The Hulk,
    it's mine, it consumes me, I try to write and it screams Why Bother, Who Cares,
    let The Famous Poet sing that sunset:
Or worse: that horrible song I've heard since childhood: **that it'll never be enough.**

The diner's closing. The chairs are being put on the tables. The rubber mats have been taken
    outside and cleaned; the Mexican girl's sweeping up; the waitress is rushing through her
    own hamburger and fries. I've finished the greasy grilled eggplant, the very well done
    fries, I'm just now finishing the second iced coffee. In the forty minutes I've been here
    I've eaten, I've written this:
Maybe it's even a poem.
I've discovered that the block is my unloveliness, my ugliness, my envy
Mine own envy

(211) Why I Can't Write (cont).

Like the Famous Poet, I'm a gay American, alive & well & writing today
I might (still) want what I think he has, though I know I don't truly know what he does have
Maybe I'll never make the Times Book Review, never get the cash advance, the displays at B&N,
But I still have that need to write; I still have that need to discover. The path, the discovery,
      the magic: it's in the writing. That's what I'll need to do if I'm to find it at all:

"Your best work is yet to come," said the tarot card reader, and I believe her.
I'll go on. I'm curious to discover what I have yet to say.

> Tarrytown - Croton - Hawthorne, NY
> July - August 2003

(212) Poem: For The Man With The Scar on His Neck
for DS

So we walked along Second Avenue, you and I, walking slowly, like old Jews walking,
Nikki, on skates, fifteen, a slim, sweet bumblebee, floating around us.
They let you out the hospital an hour earlier, 'cause you showed you were free of the anesthetic;
Unshaven; a neck held together with a line of silver staples. To 10th Street: for ramen, and yaki soba.

They told you it was like granite, the carotid now opened, the red life flowing freer, now
You'll stay at Linda's for a day or so, then back to the new apartment: Long Beach.
You'll be working by next week, pushing, still; judges rolling their eyes and cautioning you;
They know how you're playing this game. You do, too. You still seem to enjoy it—a little.

You & I, you tell me, we'll never retire—we'll work 'til the end. I think we will.
So much we drank, and gambled, and pissed away, and lost. But fuck it, we'd do it again.
('Course, we'd do it right, next time.) You & I, we'll play a little, yet:
But it ain't the same as it was. ODAAT, today. It's 25 years, for you. And there's Nikki, too.

"So when will I see you?" "You'll see me when you see me."
That seems to work, still. We've now got four new months of Highlights,
Linda's play, the end of the month. Maybe I'll take you along on one of my trips;
Both got miles to go, before we sleep. Seems t'be working: 'cause we're not crazy at the same time.

So listen to your Basie, your Pizzarellis, and breakfast, again, that terrace, St. Martin, next December:
Friendship's gifts. Each of us, always alone; my hand in your hand. The connection still matters.

Croton-on-Hudson, NY
January 2003

212.

(213) Ganymede's Song

Zeus, on his travels, saw the loveliest youth
Turned himself into an eagle and snatched him up
Brought him to Mount Olympus; made him his cup-bearer

When it first happened, I didn't understand
The beak sharp on the back of my neck, the talons cutting into my smooth bare shoulders
The eagle took me to a rough outcropping in the rock, laid me down, removed my tunic
A trembling, naked youth; the powerful, lustful bird before me

He took me that first time as that magnificent eagle;
I gave myself completely to the power of the god
My beauty given over to the pleasure of the god
My beauty an offering to the lust of the god

He shifted-shape, after, took the form of a warrior,
Holding me, caressing me, taking me again, the man loving the youth,
I felt a love I never had, never could've had, with a mere mortal
Surrendering, for all time: to the service of my Lord.

Later, he wrapped me in his arms; all I could feel was a whirling, a dizziness, a blindness;
Mount Olympus. And I understood, beyond words, that this would be my holy task.
When my Lord craves wine, I lovingly bring the cup to his lips:
And I live for those moments that his lust rises for me.

My body now only for the pleasure of Zeus; blessed among mortals,
I dwell at his feet; the loving cup-bearer of the chief of the gods.

Graymoor - Croton, NY
November 2003

213

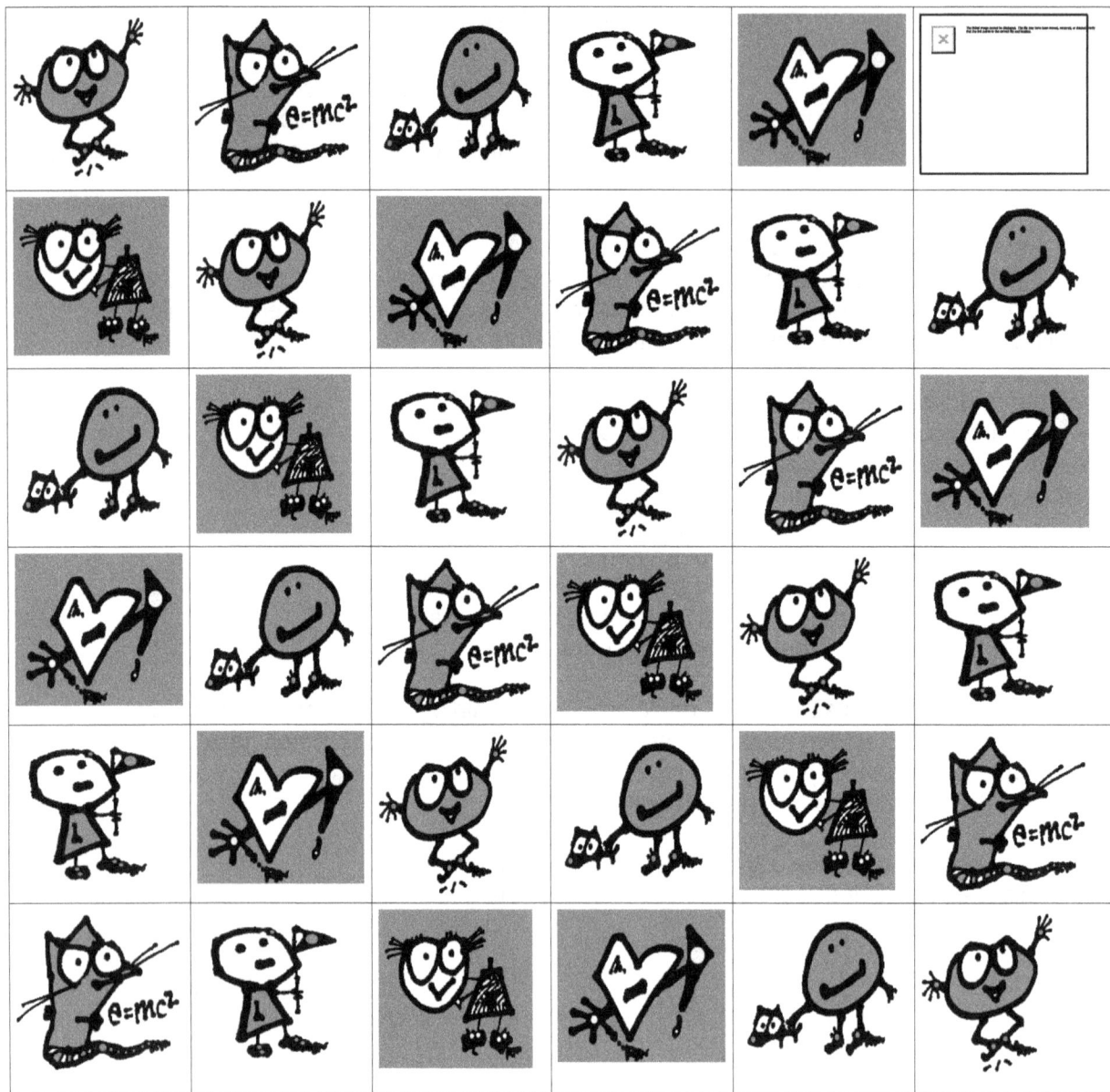

(214) empowerment sestina

214.

(215) Empowerment Sestina

In the darkness of the white woods, I remember gratitude.
I've learned that the gifts of this life come from more than intelligence,
That the heart needs to be opened with the grace of compassion,
That clinging weakens, that the way is of non-attachment,
That I've a responsibility to live my life with integrity,
That the heart will doubtlessly, deeply fall: its passion;

But it can be glorious to live fully, the dangerous depths of heart's passion,
And when it fades, as it does, perhaps it can be replaced with gratitude.
The separations of mind, body, spirit are false, we must strive for integrity
And a measure of understanding, coming in part from our intelligence.
But it's important to remember all we see will fade, to remember non-attachment,
And since all fades we might step back, and work on developing compassion.

For the heart can be gentled, quieted, with even a drop of compassion,
Though desire will of course return, with all of its splendid burning passion.
If we can remember the non-judgment of the witness, the serenity of non-attachment,
The gift of such conscious thought is the sun-shining blessing of gratitude.
All of this has nothing to do with clinging to, or using our intelligence,
It's a result of letting go, and of accepting our integrity.

For we're not separate, not a patchwork quilt; rather, we do have individual integrity,
And need to know we're not alone, we're part of the all; to remember compassion,
And to use the gifts we've been given, correctly; that the proper use of our intelligence
Is to create the new, to build a new Eden, the possibilities of this world; our passion
May be channeled, to reduce suffering, to feel other's needs more, even their gratitude;
But I know what seems like service is really not: remembering, non-attachment.

If we're caught in the illusion of doing, even doing good, we forget non-attachment,
Which leads to suffering, to the hideous dramas created by fear; we lose our integrity;
We may think we're serving but we think too highly of ourselves, we lose our gratitude,
We forget that it's not our doing, it's just being done; we need to be reminded of compassion,
To remember that the heart, the mind, the body, will always be swayed by its passion,
And the way to transcend such states is given both by wisdom and intelligence.

215.

(216) Empowerment Sestina (cont.)

Though it's a limited attribute, we all need a measure of intelligence,
But more, it'd be better if we lived more in non-attachment.
To hear Springsteen or Dylan sing their truth with unfailing passion
Brings ever-new respect for these heroes; their integrity.
The abandoned child, the fighters, Kosovo, Brooklyn; reminding us of compassion;
Our lives enriched, these many blessings: remembering, gratitude.

Even a life of gratitude, punctuated by truth beyond the scope of intelligence,
Falls short if we neglect compassion. If we forget the emptiness of non-attachment.
The integrity I'm striving for. The passion of creating a rich, full, useful life.

Westchester County, NY
August - September 2004

(217) Barry's Song

The photo's of Barry Weinbaum, in shades and a graduate's gown
Big smile, two thumbs up, graduating from Bennington, June '82.
But he never got the diploma 'cause he owed the school $600,
And that matters little 'cause he was strangled, thrown onto 3rd Street, July 9.

Barry paid his own way through the expensive college, partial scholarship and selling cocaine,
Had an alcoholic mother who beat him, a father who barely knew him. On his own since 17,
He was a charmer, personable, bright, editor of the newspaper, captain of the softball team;
He wrote of Prince Hal, who *"walked between worlds."* Barry too knew both East Village and Vermont,

Knew his smile and the right attitude could work, wherever. A chameleon, a schmoozer,
He knew how to get by. Needing cash for his expensive tastes, he drove down from Vermont,
Had a beer and a cheeseburger at Pete's Tavern, left his old car near Gramercy Park,
Walked to meet the man, 4th Street and Avenue D. The body was found that night, a block away.

Bennington friends searched for him, first as missing; then they tried to find the killer;
To them, the cops seemed mostly uninterested. No suspects were mentioned in the article.
Money buys things, it's a valuable tool; selling coke's a fast easy way to make fast easy bread,
But there are dangers when you piss people off, justified or not. Barry lived fast; also died, very fast.

He chose the expensive school, the clothes, the trips, wanted all the toys this wealthy world offers:
 A big confident smile, front page of the Times; dead, at 22. His brief, bitter taste of fame.

Reference:
"Life and Death of a Campus Drug Dealer,"
by Marcia Chambers, New York Times, September 5, 1982.

Croton-on-Hudson, NY
February 2004

DAVID'S BOOK

The title is, **"David's Book."**

So: who else should it be for?

(223) The Chosen Poems: Toward an Explanation

for DS

I've known you, I'm guessing, almost 25 years now; I'd
Sat with you at meals and meetings, at concerts and funerals, and certainly at the beach;
Stayed with you in hotels in Del Ray and AC; stayed at your judge's apartment, Rockaway,
Spoke to you, week after week, from 12th Street, from Croton, and now from Pooler

It's called a friendship. We share interests--Basie. Sinatra. The rooms. Lusts.
Our opinions not superimposable--politics differ, big-time. But music beats that easy,
And it's mostly the music that's kept the connection strong. Highlights, JVC, Waterloo, and
The Bechet at the Lighthouse that I never got to. Now a long way from NYC; gotta let it go.

Wanted to do something for the day, looked through files of poems, some never-seen by anyone,
Others, occasional poems. Think of friends passed, of friends still around--hell, life goes on. It must.
I jumped to the south this past spring, today's been a rainy GA Saturday, a great indoor day, with old
Tapes of Schwartz, with Torme, Renzi, Leonhart and Pizzarelli--and I even got some writing done.

Need to finish up this package, books & catalogs, CD's, audio tapes, a video, clippings from the files,
And now ***David's Book***, too. It ain't much, I know, it ain't even rock & roll, but I like it; it is what I do:

And so, again, I wish you well. Keep doing what you're doing, what you've been doing:
Somehow, it all seems to be working. ODAAT.

Pooler, GA
July 2007

223.

(224) Poem for My Denial

The cold new dawn of the bitter realization
The last unhappy day of the hideous twisted journey

Slammed into the sidewalk, the rubble of my sheltered emotions
The world of laughter, of the sweet ordinary: never connecting, never mine
This the sour perception, the sad reflection, the horror,
Alone, apart, ashamed: *"as it must always be;"*
Beaten, finally, by the dark power, the killing disease

The shaking crawl into the welcoming rooms
The slow beginning, the subtle shifts, toward total change of self: recovery.

The discovery of warmth and wholeness, beyond mere anger and fear
The movement toward acceptance; by others, more, by myself;
The mirror now giving intimations of simple humanity, of clear-eyed sobriety;
Nothing lasts forever when the goal's a day at a time.
Living, the miracle of our program: finally, humbly, in the grace of God.

NYC
October – November 88

(225) Independence Day, New York City

Muslim in paper-thin robe, turban, sandals, corner payphone:
She passes, badly dyed red hair, lipstick a scarlet burn, torn black stockings,
      too tight black dress; the same sandals

* * * * * * *

Yuppie: *"his sunburned face matches his convertible's interior."*

* * * * * * *

The Korean grocer's anxiety, jealously guarding his American dream
Next block, his son, also on duty, casually eats Wise potato chips

* * * * * * *

Tall, elegant woman, long black skirt
She bends to read a menu

* * * * * * *

Dark, fortyish, thickly-built jogger
The bent, gray, slow-moving man

* * * * * * *

"'S'cuse me, I don't mean to be forward, but…"
Wrinkled dowager in trendy pastels, instinctively fearful
"You really look great!" A smile, her relaxation;
An easy, unimportant lie.

* * * * * * *

Wm. C. Greenburg Jr. Desserts, Inc.;
Only three black workers remain

* * * * * * *

He knocks wood whenever he can;
He refrains at Trump's latest dig.

* * * * * * *

Homeless man, in doorway next to David K's,
Carefully reads a newspaper in the dimming light.

* * * * * * *

The cardboard in the shadows, the dirty black eyes, the tiny voice
"Please help"

* * * * * * *

The silver-haired ladies; the matted-down poor

* * * * * * *

The desperation, her homeless eyes
The cash machine

* * * * * * *

The Chrysler Building: its lightning, its vision

* * * * * * *

"Gee, I'd hate to be driving in this--"
Cop on every corner, five on 57th

* * * * * * *

The sleeper on cardboard:
866 Second Avenue

* * * * * * *

Sweating hard now into the humidity
Vomit near the sewer at the corner, 48th and 2nd

* * * * * * *

"Th' diff'rence b'tween the crowd and the mob?
I guess it has t'do with which side y'r on."

* * * * * * *

Blocked traffic car horns, the explosions above us
Loud laughter in Spanish

* * * * * * *

The spectacle, the reason we're all here
"AHHHHHHHH..............."

* * * * * * *

The sophisticated, expectant, insatiable crowd
The pleased smile; the stifled yawn
"Ay, que linda!" *"Sarah! Over here, Sarah!"*

* * * * * * *

Traffic stalled for many blocks
The scream of sirens, the promise of showers
The shock of two dozen firecrackers--a willowy blonde in black

NYC/July 89

(228) "Why Lisa Is Lovable"

"…who loves himself loves me who loves myself."
--Allen Ginsberg, 1956

Because you have the courage to ask for such support

Because you're possessed of physical beauty unmatched
    (Persistent image of you in black stockings, black garter belt, black cotton
    warm contrast to smooth tan skin, to blondness at head, at lovely crotch)

Because that image sweetly pleases, filling me with desire to stroke you, kiss you,
    to take away your pain

Because I see you lying between Dave and Peggy, accepting the love you'd needed,
    the love you'd been able to ask for, the love you deserve--the marvelous image,
    the teaching of love!

Because I've looked the deep silence behind your eyes, know the depth of being beyond
    the lovely surface

Because I've seen you give love to those who couldn't yet trust it in themselves,

Because you teach openness by example, as you reveal your own imperfections,

Because your self-image is no longer dependent on your father's opinions,

Because living in friendship is an absolute, noble commitment,

Because in talking with you I feel safe, supported, accepted,

Because talking on the phone with you is hopeful, and easy,

Because above all else is a willingness to give, and to grow;

Because you trusted me enough to ask for these loving words.

NYC/October 90

228.

(229) For Joyce
via Ken

Your smile a warm beach at low tide,
A gentle spirit, quiet goodness;
Shadows, darkness, hurtful storms:
Passing moods. Sad imprints remain.

As giving lover, as special friend
You fire my days; you glory my nights.

NYC—NJ
February 91

(230) Soulmate
for Ronnie

Gray dark rain, black curtain, drenching heaviness:

Imagined. Our reality's different, it's better;
  A bank of caring friends to draw from
  The material struggle, strangely, some success
  The river of heartbeat, the space between breath,
   the silence behind knowledge, we know, we're comforted;

So close. Needing only that one.
  He who uniquely fills your void, as you fill his,
  Unavoidable! Blossoms exploding exactly when right…!
  Trusting the Master, who knows our needs, desires;
   His holy time

You and I caught, this horribly human process
  Aware: that clinging must lose its death-like grip,
  That illusion and truth the same cosmic coin, that when
  Acceptance becomes our living heart, our deep sigh,
   Our single point of being

The lover we're finally ready for smiles gently,
  And asks permission to meet us.

NYC
June 92

230.

(231) "Yo, Pops!"
for Charlie

Just another day. But one worth noting--in remembrance:
       The house dominated by women, pharmaceuticals for the soda jerk,
       Charley Waffles the screamer, chocolate sodas across from Bon Soir,
       The hookers, the cocaine, the emptiness which follows, always;
        "I can't sit on the chair, I've only got three days;"

Just another day. But one of health & sobriety--in service:
       The little girls who cluster around you, remaining untouched,
       Phone calls through the evening, healing with laughter, talking your truth,
       Living the program, sometimes *"the only Big Book someone gets to see;"*
       A family restored, the glorious grandchild--your link to the future;

Remembering the past and letting it go; accepting the future one day at a time,
But living fully today, delis and doctors, auditions and meetings: living your recovery:

Your life today--healthy, useful, reasonably sane & happy:
Creating, daily, this life: a life of worth, of hope, of joy. Just another day.

Graymoor, NY
September 99

231.

(232) "Who's Got It Better Than Us?"

for David

A warm Tuesday afternoon, middle o'May, the boardwalk, Atlantic City,
Just walked out of Showboat, $150 to the good & *"Muskrat Ramble"* still in our ears.
Join the crowd of pensioners this fine day, a couple of hearings set for tomorrow, but nothing today;
Cool breeze off the ocean, small win in the pocket; a hot dog, a cold drink; a good day, a good friend.

I've heard pieces of your story often, some parts still too painful, no need to pick up that knife,
So can't know the eight years before '84, know only the surface, Vegas or New Orleans whore-stories
Can't know the hurt of the first daughter, but know the shining pride & love & joy received from Nikki,
Glorious child, giving meaning to it all, keeping you from becoming the bum on the beach with a bottle.

"Not all crazy at the same time," words you & I live by, laugh by, keeping us reasonably together,
Japanese dinners before Highlights, the commonality of our pleasures, jazz, old jokes, various lusts,
And meetings, and meetings, and meetings, and working & living the program as best as we can;
 $150K in debt, no lovers in our lives, and you telling me: *"Who's got it better?"* And you're **right.**

If friendship is a blessing, a gift, a necessity for a healthy, useful, constructive life,
I'm grateful: the blessing of our connection. It's an honor to call you friend.

Croton-on-Hudson--Hawthorne, NY
July 99

232.

(233) For David, at Seventy

Actually, you're older than that
'Cause Americans miscount

'Cause we celebrate our *first* birthday
After we've been on the planet for a year

So you've actually *completed* seventy years
'Course, try explaining *that* one to Social Security

Meanwhile, I'm somewhat at a loss for words
While I listen to the tape you gave me, the sampler,
The sweet Dixieland *"Curse of an Aching Heart,"* with Bucky's *"Big Noise"* upcoming
Looking forward to seeing Compo at St. Peter's on Sunday; to seeing you, too

Hot ol' toothless Alberta Hunter, *"Age Ain't Nothin' but a Number,"*
Ain't got nothin' on you

So much we share, the range of this life, the heights, the depths, the laughter;
And the day has passed. And we're both still here, still in the midst of it all, still walkin' this planet

I wish you health, longer life, stability, sanity, even serenity, in the midst, these Madnesses, our lives;
One day at a time. Even the special ones, ODAAT. But not finished; more before us to do:

Stay with us. Keep on.

Croton-on-Hudson, NY
August 2000

233.

(234) Since 1970
for Larry

It's all about the jazz…
>Sonny Fortune at Boomer's, Illinois Jacquet on 58th Street
>Duvivier and Cheatham at Highlights

It's all about the jazz…
>Tito Puente, Ray Barreto, Celia Cruz; blindfold tests on West End Avenue
>Smoky Schaefer concerts at Wollman Rink

It's all about the jazz…
>The only white boy at Gil Scott-Heron: *"I'm a mulatto;"* the angry brothers laughing
>Black urban poetry years before rap

It's all about the jazz…
>Tennis in Baldwin with pitchers afterward; the Mini Cinema, Tower Records and J&R
>Radio City and Highlights at NYU, and Pace

It's all about the jazz…
>The real Ray Lundin ripping up the notebook; Harry Katzan and FORTRAN on punch cards
>Texaco, Pfizer, Levitton and the City of New York

It's all about the jazz…
>Newport and Kool and JVC and Ken Burns, Peggy and Anita and Sassy and Ella
>Dizzy and Dexter and Stan and Basie

It's all about the jazz…
>Closing the bar after we'd dropped off the girls; asthma, diabetes, and now pneumonia
>A loving partner in Ruth Ann, twenty years, now

It's all about the jazz…
>All the changes a lifetime brings: the growth; the continuance; the collections
>A friendship lasting more than thirty years:

It's always, always, always: it's all about the jazz.

East Brunswick, NJ/August 2002

(235) Rules
for Linda

Theater's about collaboration, it's more than just the writing; it can't be completed, alone.
But the playwright begins with the ideas, the image, the information,
Creates the characters, the context, the conflict: a mother. A daughter.
A gentleman caller. And Nine-One-One.

A Sunday afternoon, fifty of us, friends, family, theater types;
A staged reading, the well-known actress, her name above the title,
The first reading of a new creation, this new play, this babe, entering the world:
Linda's words, images, ideas; Linda's vision. Becoming alive. The process of theater.

You've created this mother, this daughter: *real.* Living. Breathing. Annoying sometimes,
But annoying 'cause they're *real.* Showing our times: our reactions to divorce, to dating:
To Harold, and his plugs. To the skydiver, grabbing her breasts. To the thugs in the Metro:
The denial of the heritage. Fear. Passion. The choices we face: these, our difficult times.

Now the real drama begins: some rewrites (minor). More workshops, if you can.
And the money: *that's* the hard part. Finding the backers: life ain't like *The Producers*.
But it's good to have a rabbi, someone who's been around, someone who'll lend support;
It's good that she believes in the work. It's even better when she stands to gain, too.

The process of this art needs the audience, need the circle, for it to be complete.
A good, strong beginning. This new voice (*yours*): a working, thinking, feeling playwright.

Croton – Hawthorne NY
June 2003

235.

(236) Reality Check: No, You're Not Crazy
for DS

Ranges of madness through our most comfortable culture
It's too terrible, it's too dangerous, not to laugh

"She wants me to come over for Passover."
OK.
"But then she calls back and tells me that she wants to invite him along too."
Oh—kay.
"And I tell her no."
OK.
"And she doesn't understand."
Yes.
*"She doesn't understand that I don't want to sit at a table and have dinner
        with the guy who's fucking my wife."*
Ex-wife.
*"Yeah. But doesn't she understand that if I have to meet the guy,
        I'll nod, I'll be civil. But I don't want to spend an evening with her
        & this guy & **know** what's going to happen later."*
I understand.
"Yeah. So I told her no, and hung up."
OK.
*"I mean, I'm not that modern kind of guy. I know what she does. I can't stop her.
        I don't **wanna** stop her. But does she have to rub my face in it…?"*
No.
"So she calls me back later and apologizes."
OK.
"She didn't realize how I felt."
OK.
(Silence.)
"…You know this is gonna happen again."
Sure.
"So—am I crazy, or what?"

Hawthorne, NY/April 2003

(237) Move A Muscle, Change A Thought

These mood changes I put myself through
Self-knowledge: should know better, by now.
Got caught. In the Friday night misdirection, my lateness:
Translated as a no-show. The repeat of misdirection. Annoyance. And the bitter taste of:
> *another evening: shot.*

This sourness I stay with, the weekend wasted: small, necessary things.
Riding twice, into the heart of it. Uncared for; happy, in the midst of the uncaring crowds.
Just another pedestrian, Bleeker, Thompson to Bowery. Past Planned Parenthood, past
The darkened storefront where Yipster Times once lived. Now the European-style bar:
> the big-screen soccer match.

The babe in red pajamas: just learning how to walk. He'll be 20 when I'm 70; if we both make it.
The cars roll north & south on Bowery. Two female lovers share coffee, the table by the window.
Can't get stuck in the sourness. My limited energy, tar pits of worthless, self-defeating dullness:
Move. Change. Do. The what doesn't matter, the power's in the doing:
> the smallest action flicks the mood-switch.

More than belief: experimentally proven, over & over again: remember: Do.
The sourness will return. Accept. Act. It loses its power; we move on. We do move on.

NYC - Newark - Phoenix, AZ
February 2003

(238) Bittersweet Pain
for Kathleen

Sometimes I try to imagine what it'd be like,
"I don't really have to go to all those meetings,"
Maybe I can really handle it now;
Been so long since I've gotten high

So much I've missed out on, these last 20 years,
Never did Ecstasy, never did crack,
Never did enough psychedelics,
Still miss that sweet dopey goofiness, the pot-high

Think of the *ganga* clubs in Amsterdam
Think of partying deep through long nights in Vegas
Maybe I'm not that alcoholic, that addict, maybe I'm not, anymore
Maybe I could handle it all, this time…I know the program so well

Such illusions must be smashed, says the literature
But my process is slower, the method: just letting it all go;
Can't deny I play with these dangerous thoughts
Need to use the tools and think this stuff through

"It's easier to stay sober than to get sober,"
First heard from old Frank, PAX, so many years ago;
Just as true today. Need to work this daily, work to keep this gift,
Need to practice this, harder. Need to keep giving it away.

I need to keep walking these steps, keep living this program:
"Everything to lose and nothing to gain." Stay this path; live it, today.

Graymoor - Croton, NY
January 2005

238.

(239) Notes: on the Dissemination of The Files
for David, Ranger, Raul, Monday Night, and Ryn

I know how it all started: a single Joel Oppenheimer column, The Voice, '69,
Carried with me, my first trip to the West, 1973:
>*"the clouds coming down to meet the people"*
>*"I just want to have a book with the poems in it before I die"*

Scraps of paper, newspapers, magazines: *"reading I could do while watching television;"*
Neatly clipped, dated, referenced, Xeroxed by the thousands, shipped Rockaway to NOLA
To Rockaway to Tucson to LA to Rockaway to East Village to Morrisville to Croton;
Billions of words, dormant, unread for years: waiting

The next move: upcoming. No longer makes sense to carry it all,
But an outright dump denies thirty years, my inner life.
Now dismantling, dumping much; actually easy, letting so much go,
But save that Mike Lupica column. Save that interview with Groucho.
Save that "gay cancer" article from '83.

Grateful for the blessings of friends, different spirits, different tastes, I can now offer:
>Sinatra and Hyman for David,
>Leonard Cohen for the Ranger,
>Santiago Baca for the Warrior,
>The card game for New Roc Monday night, and
>Our all-American murderers, for the poet now in Tucson.

This week I flew LA-Chicago-Savannah, had a good Swiss burger on GA Highway 21;
Tomorrow I'll look for the apartment. I'm expecting to move here by spring.
Strong-armed moving men will carry my boxes, heavy with other people's words;
It's not over. I haven't abandoned the work, just let it go a bit, just staying unattached;
Always meant to be fodder for the writing. But what I could never explain:
>**it was all just so much fun.**

Savannah, GA – Croton, NY
March – April 2007

(240) Life and Times
for DS

> *"I come from a family of long livers.*
> *I had an uncle had a liver that was **this long**."*
> *--old Vaudeville joke*

When you were 10 the Nazis showered London with death

When you were 20 you were readying yourself for Korea

When you were 30 Jack was fucking Marilyn into the New Frontier

When you were 40 I was a year away from daily drugging and drinking

When you were 50 you'd been dry for four years

When you were 60 you'd take baby Nikki to Potpourri

When you were 70 we'd learned that Y2K was a wisp in the breeze

Now you're 77
       Still working every day, still worrying the hearings, the bills
       Still on the beach, ogling *("you should **see** what this one has on")*
       Still a divorced, sober, hardworking father

You and I, you once told me, we'll never retire, we'll work 'til the end
You and I, we're still working. Still good to have you as my friend.

Pooler, GA
July 2007

240.

ILENE'S BOOK:

POEMS and

PHOTOGRAPHS

Y'know, this the third time I've had to say it:

The *title* is **Ilene's Book:**

Who else could it be for???

Phil, Ilene & Roz, Brooklyn, NY, circa 58

(244) Roz, Phil & Ilene, East Brunswick, NJ, October 93

(245) Introduction: For the Baby at Fifty

Fifty's a milestone, I think; others have passed it: your sister, your brother,
Your husband, for three; but it remains a number of import, nevertheless,
Means other things to each, I suppose; for me, it's the knowledge that
I ain't 22 anymore, so I can't—and don't—live that way, today.

There'll be a Sunny Palace party; sorry, I won't be there,
My life's allowed for different cities, from the West to the East Village;
Now it's the charming south. I'll have just returned from an SF - LA week,
Besides, there'll be a healthy, noisy crowd. This book will be my stand-in.

Started thinking of something special for you, after Barry's e-mail,
I've given you more lipstick than you & your friends could ever use,
But for 30 years I've been both chemist and poet, and
Now seems about the right time for a book for you.

The photos scanned in, from the large box here in the Pooler apartment.
        Many of the poems are new:
18 poems—a deliberate choice. An attempt at a vision, your life—
        the baby sister—at 50.

Charlotte, NC – Newark, NJ
May 2008

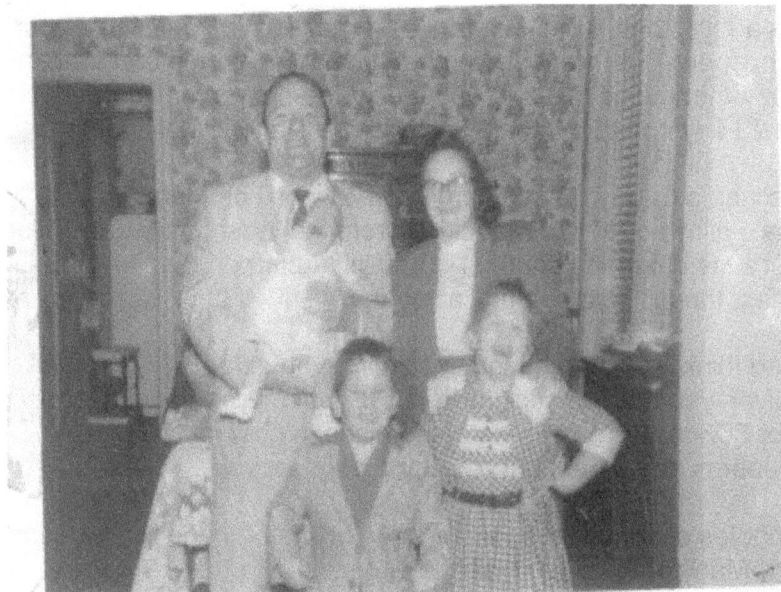

(246)   Family, Brooklyn, NY, 58

(247) Our Father

Talking about it now, seems strange to friends: we never had a family vacation;
I hear my father's voice—"*You want a vacation? Walk to the beach!*"
That was my understanding, his rationale, buying that house, the suburbs;
Don't now know how much I heard, how much I made up: our near-silent father.

Never spoke his childhood, never spoke his army years, save the one story:
Only man in the regiment to lift a barber chair (I believed 'til I was eight).
After Mom died, saw photos of him in Marseilles, probably '46 or '47;
Full head of hair, polished army boots, big relaxed grin: showing off his gold tooth.

The story was that they were first cousins, that Mom wrote to him during the war,
His visa gave him five days in the US; they went to Manhattan, were married by the judge.
He split for Havana; three months later, back to stay, they had the (real) Jewish wedding;
He started working, his father-in-law; didn't work. Then came the shoe factory. And the kids.

From a little town, the Russian-Polish border, to a wife, a family, a house at the beach;
Our father lived his American dream. Just wish he could've been able to tell us about it.

East Brunswick, NJ
May 2008

247.

(248) Blanche, Arverne, NY, April 83

(249) For Bleimeleh

I visited the graves last Monday, didn't tell you,
Hoped to spare you some unnecessary guilt--a burden you might foolishly create for yourself.
It's only a symbol, the life they lived together, the children they parented, the lives we have now;
What mattered was her good life. And she still lives, and laughs; the memories of her kids.

A hearing-aid wearing Jew, born and raised in Richmond, but
Once she saw NYC, there was no turning back. Koch Bros.Groceries grew in Brooklyn,
As the family followed the stubborn daughter. And Blanche married Alex in '48, and
Rosalyn was born in '50, when they lived on Alabama Ave. And two more followed.

So important, for her, driving, knew it was necessary, or be stuck in the Rockaway wilderness.
Soon after the move, she discovered Mah Jongg; except for Alex, was the great love of her life.
It all made sense to her: husband, kids, the car giving freedom of movement, Mah Jongg;
Smoked for 43 years, stopped, too late. At the end, the cough was more than just a cough.

When Dad died, we sold the house; she had her apartment, Shore Front,
Looking out at the ocean she loved. *"A woman of valor,"* the books say.
     We always knew her as Mom.

Lincolnshire, IL
May 2008

249.

(250) Family, Oceanside, NY, December 84

(251) Sisters
for Roz and Ilene

When we moved to Rockaway, the two sisters shared a room,
Eight years seemed a lifetime, ages five and thirteen.
Ilene always had her bed at the far side of the room, made it tough when Roz
Divided the room in half; to get out she'd have to crawl out the window

Two sisters growing up together, blackberry brandy at the beach,
Masked to Mom as food poisoning. Roz and I blew smoke in your face,
You talked incessantly of Holly Hobby—while we did or didn't see green.
You got your own room when Roz married what's-his-name—she returned, after the divorce.

You married Barry, took the Staten Island apartment, while Roz held Tim's coat, then married.
You bought your own house, Meadow Road, East Brunswick; it became our *Chateau Gray.*
So many weekends, Roz & Tim & I visiting, concerts, dinners, holidays, AC,
Sometimes some tension: personalities, closeness, anger. I stayed my 36 hours & fled.

A long history, two sisters, still close, closer-now-than ever; time continues to pass;
Cells allow more-frequent contact (too much for Tim). Stable, healthy: the sisters, continuing.

Lincolnshire, IL
May 2008

251.

(252) Phil Feigning Drunkenness, Arverne, NY, October 81

(253) Poem from a Brother

You adored me as a teen. *"You're my Big Brother."*
Never felt worthy. Through high school, scared, set apart;
Wearing out *"I Am A Rock"* in my darkened bedroom. Terrified, lonely:
You knew none of this. You loved what you believed I was.

In college, I drank and smoked. Tried speed once, a Saturday night,
Went into your room to say goodnight; talked nonstop for 45 minutes.
The drunkenness scared you; eventually did me, too:
Now the better way, more than 23 years. One day at a time.

Calling from Hollywood, talking to you and Roz; unseen for almost two years,
You two'd grown closer, and at 20, your demand clear: treat you as an adult.
Years later, that closeness still strong; me, in my travels, honoring that;
And us? A healthy, adult relationship. Sometimes in 36-hour increments.

Family always the constant, family both *"pushing, even installing our buttons."*
Real caring; minor annoyances. The reality of family; the reality of love.

Charlotte, NC – Newark – East Brunswick, NJ
May 2008

253.

(254) Ilene, Brooklyn, NY, February 61

(254) Ilene, Arverne, NY, July 63

(255) The Baby
for Ilene, on her birthday

Strange to think of you as woman now

I fly in the face of truth
What I know to be truth is not what I feel

Looking at photographs
The snowsuit, the tricycle
Twenty years ago, and more, these

Today you sit in meetings on Park Avenue, discuss million-dollar accounts
Today you run the household, a married woman, you fight & laugh, friends & family
You know that I know you and love you as the person you are today

But I close my eyes:
The snowsuit, the tricycle

My sister: 'til the end of our days.

NYC
June 85

255.

(256) Birthday Poem: The Baby at Thirty
for Ilene

It seems, somehow, you're no longer the child: instead,
      you're the long-suffering wife and worker,
      the worrier over dollars and doctor's visits,
      the bright balancer of the sometimes-shaky books,
      the anticipator of the better life-to-come;
Amazingly, somehow, you're a grown-up:
Hard to believe...

Especially when I screen my internal video,
See the black-and-white image of the snow-suited two-year-old,
      the giggling seventh-grader's posters of Cassidy and Spitz,
      the nervous bride on her one special day,
      the new homeowner of the not-too-distant past;
I've watched you, been a part of you
As you're a necessary part of me

And tonight, at the intimate dinner, there'll be laughter, hugs, hope
      talk of friends and co-workers, both pro and con
      of the new work done on the house, and the yet-to-be-done
      of the true, tight bonds of family, which endure, still
      of the desire for that easier, happier life, which waits for you:
Today is a milestone, yes, but it's neither beginning nor end:
The road ahead is wide, clear and bright. This day; this day, is yours.

NYC –NJ
June 88

256.

(257) Ten Years Together
for Ilene & Barry

The marriage knows its living heart,
Past passions, hoarse angers, quiet dullness;

Its strength a breathing, growing, two-centered love:
The force which orders the universe;

The force giving purpose to your days.

NYC
July 92

(258) Belated Poem: Numerology II
for Ilene

You're 35. 3 + 5 = 8.

Much late for your day, but still with love I bring:

An English rose, a Chinese box,

The bath of soft bubbles, the wicked loofah,

Practical plastic for your money-savings,

The pan to try the new and different,

Words of bright women like yourself,

The obligatory duck, here in copper backed with magnet:

Enjoy, use, play with 'em: small deservings, for a good woman.

NYC
October 93

258.

(259) Mother's Day Poem
(for my sister's mother-in-law)

In time, the family extends,
Grandma's boys, cousins to cousins,
Even to those beyond warm blood:
Tied by living vows, by continuing choice.

Her power is the ancient one,
Of home and hearth, of Sarah, Rebecca,
The constant center, the ever-present, stable heart:
A woman's strength: the necessary factor.

She was a girl, once, courted gently in Brooklyn,
Girl became mother, raised boy and girl, healthy, strong.
Grandchildren now, retirement, cruises:
Today we honor the woman: deserved respect, honest love.

East Brunswick, NJ
May 94

259.

(260) Belated Poem
for Ilene

What we are comes from the glorious ocean,
  from silent pulls of the Maiden, the dark-reflecting moon,
  from our ancestral home, the harsh gritty sands of Rockaway,
  from the choices we make, daily, throughout our lives,
  from the choices we live, throughout our lives

Who we are comes from Blanche & Alex, and before,
  from the blood-karma of our heritage, culture and Law,
  from lost Polish *shtetls* to Richmond and New York, New York,
  from the choices we make, daily, throughout our lives
  from the choices we live, throughout our lives

How we are comes from our daily struggle,
  from excess heat and humidity, from being caught in the rain,
  from money, doctors, in-laws, co-workers, lack of sleep & husbands,
  from the choices we make, daily, throughout our lives
  from the choices we live, throughout our lives

Know that you're my sister, my heart, a necessary part of who I am,
Know that I'm weakly human, open to selfishness, sloth, even red-hot rage,
Know that defects may be hidden in photo'd smiles, but live, always, in me, in us:
Know my love can't be questioned, it's a choice I make, daily:

What we are; who we are; how we are:
These remain the choices we must live, daily.

NYC – NJ
June – July 96

260.

(261) For The Baby: At Forty

Half-a lifetime: a good beginning.

History behind you, Rockaway, Staten Island, Lebhar-Goddamn-Friedman,
Future a light, a hope, an unknown shining brightness,
Today: Family. Friends. A day washed with sun, love & joy:

Always the baby; always, my sister; always, your own, love-filled Self:
Always.

Hamilton NJ—Morrisville PA
June 98

(262) For Barry / Of Barry

It would be better if you weren't always so busy,
Forever on call, waking at four to catch the bus,
Evenings so much time working for the Lodge, a legacy,
Falling asleep with the television on whenever you've a free moment

But still you find time for your own particular pleasures,
Fantasy baseball, the Mets in summer, season tickets for the Jets (again),
A quick trip to AC now and again, maybe staying over, maybe not,
A few vacations, cruises, Vegas, or just road trips: *bar mitzvahs* and weddings, family, friends.

But above all else you're Ilene's husband, more than twenty years, now:
Not quite Snowi's father, but you might as well be that, as well.
This remains your basic family unit, stronger even than other connections,
And your laughter and your love come from this base: its continuing solidity.

Nothing left to do but keep moving forward, have the party and tomorrow, back to work;
It's a good life, maybe a bit bumpy in spots, but nothing really unexpected;
     it all gets better. It continues, always, to improve.

Pooler, GA
May – June 2008

262.

(263) Chateau Gray

Since we sold the house in Rockaway, you were the only ones with any space,
So it became natural for the family to congregate by you, East Brunswick,
Hard by Route 18 and its diners, near the Turnpike, which led us the long way back,
Manhattan or Trenton or Croton, or through Staten Island and Rockaway, to Island Park.

I was the one who gave the house its name. One of my ill-fated trips, AC,
Saw a wood-carving stand, thought it'd be an appreciated gift.
You always welcomed family, friends: Thanksgiving, *Rosh Hashanah*, those
Long 36-hour weekends. Tim initiated the custom of the GP before meals.

Barry grew in barbeque expertise, through years of practice,
Lots of late-night living room conversations, Roz, Ilene, Phil & Snowi.
Roz & Tim would sleep upstairs, I shared my room with the computer,
The house needed work from day one: it's a process, and lately, much has been done.

Beyond the wood and the shingles, beyond the basement, the roof, the house remains alive:
Invested, the life of this family. More than twenty years: still going strong.

Savannah, GA
June 2008

(264) For the Diva, Ms. Snowi White

We've always been a family that loved dogs:
Had a cat in Rockaway 'til she had kittens, and Dad got rid of 'em all.
In Rockaway there was Champ, and Rusty, and Roz and Someone Else had Pepper;
Elvis and Sweet Pea had Roz & Tim, and now there's sweet, sweet Snowi, the Jersey girl.

She came into your lives at the time of great need, of much dull sameness,
Her glowing radiant spirit transformed the home, brought lightness and laughter to us all.
Her role was to accept the vast amount of love you both needed to give… 'course,
She became the diva. And maybe now. a little overweight, too (I don't think it's genetic).

Now it's a family of three; she's apparently involved in all family discussions,
Has her loud say at anyone walking by your quiet home.
She'll wait understandingly, attentively, each evening, for that last walk debate
And finally, always at the end of each day, she'll come upstairs to make Ahh Baby.

She is sweetness of spirit in sheddable white fur; it's no accident she came when she did;
Trust her. She may seem just a dog, but her spirit brings love, and tenderness, and joy;
        her energy completes your home.

Rincon – Pooler, GA
June 2008

264.

(265) For Ilene and Friends

You've always been social; Michelle lived down the block in Rockaway,
And you had your friends, PS 42 Q. By junior high, the groups coalesced,
Closest were Amy, Gwen, Abbie, and still Michelle;
Now it's an accidental meeting at a mall, an invitation in the mail; times change. Maybe people, too.

At Brooklyn College, you studied accounting,
Made & stayed friends with the girls of the House.
When you graduated, you all married at once, all bought homes in nearby NJ, close to each other,
Each began now a new phase; circumstances made all closer than ever.

The inner core was a gang of about 10 families, with
Friends and cousins and the Sisterhood and the Lodge, all part of this greater whole.
Times pass; schools, camp, *bar mitzvahs*; Larry graduated college earlier this year,
And now there's bowling on Saturday nights.

You created, cultivated, rich, strong, deep connections with your friends,
A family, beyond your family; it remains crucial, essential in your lives.

As times do pass; as times do change.

Richmond Hill – Pooler, GA
June 2008

265.

(266) Family, East Brunswick, NJ, October 93

(267) Birthday Poem: for the Baby at Fifty

For the most part, over the years, I'd been dissatisfied with the poems
I'd written for you: occasional poems, too short / too simple / rarely hitting the heart;
But maybe those weak poems can now be propped up by these scanned-in photos,
From the howling three-month-old to this smiling woman, living her abundant life.

Inevitable that we look back from fifty, the work we've done, the life we've lived,
Folding shirts, high school; many years at Lebhar-Friedman, now creating payroll for Tommy.
From Rockaway to Staten Island to the work still being done, your own house, East Brunswick,
From family passing to new friends being born: just the way it is. just the way it's always been

But I'd suggest something else, 'cause if *"50 is the new 40,"* you've a buncha good years left;
Your choices: how you want to spend your time.   Maybe the Sisterhood can find a new treasurer,
Or not, as you choose. Tommy's a pretty good job, it's a better commute; you can stay there,
But people change, always. Accept that, amazingly, you really are a grown-up. Your life: your choice.

Living in the midst of an extended family that loves you, that's proud of you,
        that wants only the best for you;
Enjoy the party. Enjoy the genuine love of your family and friends. And know:
        you can choose all things, your life. Each & every day.

Richmond Hill – Pooler, GA
June 2008

TOWARD A
WORKING-MAN'S POETRY:

SELECTED POEMS
2004 - 2013

(Unpublished)

(271) "To Love the Page More"

At slams the reader's the weaker stepchild
The winners are those who sing their words, fly their hips, who teach with their eyes,
Their poems carried by the voice, clear, un-miked, with passion, nuance, command:
The crowd listens hard, waits, breathless: we want to hear what's coming next

The poem lives on the tongue, but also, on the page,
Silent in quiet rooms, crowded bookstores, in library stacks, waiting,
Living as potential, pulp, and print, newly-created or centuries old,
Waiting to connect, new eyes, new mind: the first time's surprise, the thousandth reassurance

The common desires sought by reader and performer,
The slammers hypnotize the arbitrary judges. You know they're gonna win every time.
But readers claim both audience and page, and print lives longer, print stands stronger;
The poem on the page matters. As much as lime-green fire trucks. Tiramisu.
        Or the memory of her smile.

I'll read my words at opens, I'll read 'em at slams; it's rare that I'll take home any cash.
I'll send the stuff to magazines. Asking why only depresses, just keep telling myself, just keep on:

Alone at the keyboard, wrestling with the words, creating a poem:
If only for myself...if only for myself.

Croton, NY
February - March 2004

271.

(272) Dobbs Ferry Music Festival: August

I tell myself: maybe. Maybe I should try to write again
But if I write any more poems they shouldn't be about me
Not about that new insect-itch on my arm, or
That squinty eye-strain I seem to be increasingly getting, of late

Maybe it should be about that sunset,
Or the jazz behind me that brought me to this riverfront, today

Or maybe about the hyper little Pomeranian being walked by the girl in the white shorts
She's got a tattoo on her right shoulder
Brown top, long legs, brown sandals
And those very short white shorts

The dog plays with an older couple at the next bench,
And she walks away, past the miniature willow, the green grass, to the edge of the river,
Then doubles back, notes the musicians for a moment, turns, disappears into the crowd
As sunset approaches

The air's hazy, heavy, with our well-deserved August heat
Across the river the sun's dropping slowly into hills thick with trees
Sun's still **BRIGHTLY** burning but perceptively dropping now, picking up speed;
Now it's gone. A touch of orange light in that cloud, that one, just above that hill thick with trees

Maybe I don't have that need to write, maybe I've lost it, finally; but if I don't:
Who would've known the glory of this moment; of that sunset; or of her short white shorts?

Dobbs Ferry – Hawthorne, NY
August 2005

(273) Slow Clap

Waiting the 11:04 flight, Savannah to Charlotte,
Another business trip, another connection through Carolina

Plane comes in, probably an Atlanta connection,
Young soldiers, men and women, khaki camouflage and large duffel bags,
About 20 of them deplaning, walking slowly through the quiet terminal,
Heading for the buses waiting out front, Fort Stewart likely, and their next assignments

And we who were waiting, we just noted this parade, then someone started it--the slow clap,
First just the one sound, then a few more, and we meant it--*"Thank you for your service."*
The young faces looked confused--who were these people? They don't know us, can't know us;
Only walked steadily on, some allowing a shy smile or a nod, others dispassionate,
        eyes glued to the ground.

Months before, I'd seen the commercial, the slow clap for our soldiers at the airport;
The now-collective mind; life, imitating media. A vision, perhaps: our new future.

Asheville, NC - Pooler, GA
February 2009

273.

(274) West Asheville Bakery Café

Shaven-headed fellow in red Tae Kwon Do polo shirt, deep in conversation with the young girl
      with blonde dreadlocks, the locks nearly falling to her wispy waist

Cool day in Asheville, bright clean sun, just a little chilly; February

Lovemaking last night--John--and I'd only met him the night before

Two women--mother and daughter, I'm guessing--both in LSU purple, greet another
      woman who just walked in--huge smiles, deep hugs, all three women

"I wish I was on some Australian mountain range
* Got no reason to be there but I 'magine it would be some kind of change"*
Snippet of Dylan bounces through my head, in this new town

Longhaired, gray-haired woman, white flowered blouse, finishes her meal,
Leaves her purse at the table as she walks to the counter for a final purchase--trust;
Her pocket-sized orange New Testament; her copper, ergonomically-bent walking stick

Made the 12:30 meeting yesterday, then that great sandwich at Burgermeister's, nearby;
Drove downtown, ticked off at the closed storefront gallery, then saw the novelist's museum:
Damned betrayal by the body, embarrassing--but it could've been worse.

John left a message on the home phone, the number I'd given him,
We met at the café at Malaprop's, the bookstore which served me so well;
His story's intense--left a church, left a marriage, left his home, for Spirit, in Asheville;

When I asked if he were gay, it was tough for him to answer. Yes. No. Maybe. I don't know.

Japanese girl, glasses, very pretty: intensely studies the label of a blue can: Diet-Rite Cola

(275) West Asheville Bakery Café (cont.)

Another girl, early 20's, apparently also sharing a table with her mother:
      dark brown hair; thick streaks of blonde at the front; she rises, goes to the counter;
She moves so gently, so easily-freely, in her soft maroon skirt

It seems this place attracts quite a number of gentle, tender women: the one in brown
      waiting to be served, the one in the green checked blouse behind the counter

What kind of man would they want (or, would they even want a man?)
More ('cause it's all about me), how can I become the man to inspire their love?
How, when yes, I want their love, but equally, want other loves as well?

The teachers say, be honest regarding your myriad desires:
My lips upon those of the ones who would love me;
Gender, race, nationality, society; unimportant. My desire, my need: to love, spirit to spirit:

To share intense love's power, with all who empathize.
Spirit. Heart. Love. Connection.

West Asheville, NC - Pooler, GA
February - March 2009

(276) "My Poems Will Die With Me"
for Stuart

I began as the terminal outsider, deep levels of fear and desire,
Alone in my parked car, staring into the street, capturing a line or two on a white index card,
Scrawling my stuff in barrooms, high on pot & wine, wanting to sing my altered consciousness;
My first poem at 17. Stopped drinking & drugging at 28. I'm 56, as I write these lines.

Most poets--most people--die unremembered, save for a few friends;
Arrogance, of course, to think the world will remember the work.
It's only for the very few, for Homer, Dante, Rimbaud, Cavafy, Akhmatova, for Whitman
On his Brooklyn Ferry, daring us to sing, a hundred years hence--these few, these do endure!

But what of the rest of us? Even those who found a little fame, this life,
Oppenheimer known more for his *Voice* columns than the poetry,
Micheline seems now a second-rate Bukowski, a handful of books, all going out-of-print,
And me? A few poems in discarded journals, and the chapbooks. For others; but for myself, first.

I grew tired of arbitrary rejections, of the blindness of faceless editors,
Believing in myself, in the work; these did have value, beyond the whims of others.
My long lines followed my breath, became word documents, printed on heavy, wide, white pages;
Tiny books of poetry. I stopped selling 'em, 'cause no one bought 'em. Finally, I gave 'em away: gifts.

And maybe the books have gotten around, sometimes, even, as odd endings to sales calls:
Marrying poetry to pearlescence, connecting art to commerce, the (mad) scientist meeting the muse;
But these are light things, insignificant; ISBN-less, they're mere slivers on the waters of our culture:
The problem with *"Publishing Under the Radar"* is that the books are always out of range, for most.

A heart attack pseudo-scare, a little chest discomfort, my left hand tingling, oddly;
Waiting all day in the ER, Candler. Trying to finish up this poem, just in case.
Was it enough, this lifetime spent writing, trying so hard, to connect, to become:
I did show up. I contributed. People heard me, they did read me; so what if they forget. We all forget.

Fame fades. And the desire for it may fade, as well.
Buried deep in childhood history, my desire to shine, to matter, seems today still a part of me,
A burning desire, seemingly so hard to let go of, today, but clearly: I want to. Think: **LET GO.**
The heart won't attack me, today; more work to be done. Write something. Make the poem better.

Pooler - Savannah, GA/January 2010

(277) The Family at Denny's
for Ryn

The family at Denny's, Sunday afternoon.

The overweight father, bearded, glasses, late 40's, blue Hawaiian shirt,
     still wearing his hair long (remember the 70's?)

Next to him the bright, quick-witted 7-year old, glasses, pigtails,
     lively new ideas constantly flooding her mind

The babe, almost two, squirming and semi-screaming from his high chair

The mother, concentrating almost solely on the babe, as the little one
     throws his pacifier to the floor, knocks his sippy-cup over

And at the other side of the table, 14, maybe 15, a shock of red hair,
     black horn-rimmed glasses, dressed in black jeans,
     black sweater, black art-school t-shirt, her head down,
     concentrating, sketching

Perhaps a version of a family, perhaps spiritual kin: Michigan, circa 1973
Perhaps an early view: the artist, these days in Tucson

Savannah - Pooler, GA
August 2011

277.

(278) Sh'ma
("Sh'ma Yisroel Adonoi Elohenu Adonoi Echod"
"Hear O Israel: the Lord Your G-d, the Lord is One")

Five thousand years we'd wandered, homeless, hated,
Accepting that this is our due, holding on to our silent G-d
But even now, now that the homeland exists, we're still always on the verge:
Annihilation.   But maybe we're still supported by the silent G-d we still do love.

Years ago, I'd said I was more American than Jew, more New Yorker than American;
Now New York's been surrendered; it's not my homeland, today.
I don't deny the power of the star, just wish it were closer to my heart;
Recoverers talk of *"conscious contact;"* I pray for that, but don't feel it, don't know it, today.

The culture is mine, but not the foreign language,
Not the white & black externals of the Hasidim, not the mysteries of Kaballah.
An American, a Jew, wanting so much this connection, man and his G-d;
Few prayers sing to me, but this one helps me believe.

"Hear, O Israel: the Lord Your G-d, the Lord is One,"
If I can't hear, it's my own terrible fault: I need to open my heart, to open, even more:
    I need to know G-d's fiery Spirit, burning into me.

Croton-on-Hudson, NY – Cape Henlopen, DE
July 2003 – September 2012

(279) Poem Written Just Before Sleep

When I was a younger man
The words came so freely, easily; now I wait for
Themes to yield out of the darkness; desire still strong, execution seemingly lacking
I still claim the moniker of Poet, but seem in my quiet heart to be living it less

Images of the now, of cities I'd lived in, of people I've not seen for years
These the things I should be singing of, and perhaps yet I can;
The acceptance that the words came hard & fast when I was 22
I'm grateful that they still do come, even to the gray-haired, gray-beard, at 58

Maybe it makes no sense to write at all anymore,
Like carrying boxes of clippings from city to city, my many cities, my many moves; but
I still claim this as my own, this last attempt at creation of craft, of art, into the greater world;
In late nights, in aloneness, in struggling; in quiet dreams, in hopes, in visions; I see now

This remains my given path, my limited place, this true world; not an addiction but a calling,
Not a pile of papers but a continuing process, beyond age or city or time; clearly:
  the work, G-d bless, remains.

Wilmington, DE
August 2012

(280) Work Song

I really didn't want to come into work today. Really didn't.
It hit me hard in the parking lot, after driving into work, while I was parking the car, moving very slowly;
There was a Zac Brown song on the country station, didn't want to turn it off just yet. The chorus had
Something to do with *"I ain't in a hurry today"* and I wanted to be there with the band, relaxed, smiling;

I sure as hell didn't want to take my water bottle & briefcase & walk to the elevator and flash my card
At the black plastic electronic doohickey that'll beep and unlock the glass door. But I did just that,
And my boss was frowning because she'd gotten an e-mail from her boss at the meeting in Europe,
And suddenly the project that was *do it when you can* was now *"can we get the data today,"* and
"Phil, can you just do this real fast and dirty and get the information out to her today…"

I'd wanted to tell her I'd planned to prepare for next week's meeting or go back to that presentation
She'd shown me yesterday, and give her my thoughts, and comments, and suggestions,
          though I really don't think
She wanted to hear them, based on our last conversation on the subject, but no, today was the day of
Testing new pigments in nail polish, comparing the new with the standard, and I did it,
          and I e-mailed out both data & opinion… Finished…

And I know I'm luckier than most, not much heavy lifting here, management bought pizza for us today,
They pay us for this, there was even an e-mail about the promise of a bonus down the line…but
I'm bored, I'm tired, I'm frustrated…and it's only Tuesday… it's only freakin' Tuesday….

Philadelphia PA
March 2013

280.

Selected Poems: 2012 - 2015

(Unpublished)

(283) Birthday Ghazal*

for David

Twelve hours ago the clock read 4:44 as I woke myself out of bed—aging;
Now the clock again reads 4:44, Jonathan Schwartz over, I copy jazz disks & try to write

When I read *"Reality Check"* , I always say, *"this is not poetry, it's more journalism—*
It's a transcription of a phone conversation I had with my friend David."

Made another set of **David's Book**, giving 'em away to any who might show poetical interest,
While my mother's voice sings her true one-note song—*"You making any money at that?"*

Never have. Never will. But I keep the day job, as you do, these many long years; six months ago,
Hurting, you asked for *"one more summer."* Now it's August, your birthday, hazy hot Rockaway, again,

And you're still here, still driving to work, never enough hearings, somehow still always making it,
Still proud of Nikki, still dealing with Linda, the job, the life, the ocean, still living by the book.

What I want is more summers, even more winters, both the ease and the struggle; age'll beat me,
I know, but you've got that head start & I keep watching you & learning from you, how you do it,

How maybe I could make it happen, learning from our masters, Satchel & Satchmo, Sinatra, Bechet;
So many others; Silver & Linz still live; this new poem; a strengthened connection. For you, for me:
And it ain't yet over.

Wilmington DE
July 2012

 * *Ghazal: Persian form of poetry based on couplets, often including the poet's name in the final verse.*

283.

(284) Assignment: Purpose of Life Poem

"…and you think you maybe trust her; for she's
touched your perfect body with her mind."
--Leonard Cohen, Suzanne

Too many teachings in my ear, all respected.
The mythologist says that life has no meaning, that we bring our own meaning to it,
The drunks talk of being of service, while the invisible teachers proclaim life as joy;
The Zen-man, thoughtlessly, chops wood, carries water (or today, commutes to the 9-to-5, via I-95).

The many teachings, contradictory, all true, all valid,
All offering choices, possibilities, while I read, and think, and rant, and hope,
Each noble philosophy now interests me less and less. I continue to *do*, even if all seems pointless;
Some pleasure, Joy. Work. Suffering. Help others, if you can. Know that G-d lives.
Move toward approaching Him.

Is it an intellectual's game, or the basis of our lives?   Thought's a part of us, as is action, prayer, love,
Greatness, connection; a work-in-progress, always. Impossible, to complete.

Wilmington, DE
August 2012

(285) Poem of the Uncomfortable Job

Part of it, of course, is the fact that the way it is now is simply different than the way it was.
In Hawthorne, in Savannah, my bosses were confused by me—they didn't know the product line,
Nor the customers, nor their needs. I sounded like I knew what to do, and they let me do it.
I thrive when I'm left alone to do the work; ain't happening here. Micromanagement sucks.

It's not (necessarily) the bosses' faults; I have a part in it too, of course. My anger, my arrogance,
My refusal to simply go with the flow, foolishly fighting battles I can't possibly win; knowing better,
Acting differently. Acting, so many ways wrong for me; creating my own pain. I've done this before.
But I have to believe I can change all of this; that I (alone?) can create the better workspace.

Again: it's not my fault, but it must be my doing,
To *"care and feed your bosses, like any other house pet."*
Argue less over silly administrative blues, just give 'em what they want;
I wish my job meant more, but these days it's only a paycheck.

Once I met a man who had a trust fund. Not me; not my family;
A working man, the son of a working man; just do the job. Don't bitch; it only weakens. Move forward.

Wilmington – Cape Henlopen, DE
September 2012

285.

(286) Belated Poem: Six Birthdays in May

for Ron, Ryn, Judy, Mary, Parand, & Nancy

Some of my friends, I've lost track of, I guess
Two cards were returned to me last year
It's my fault, I know, should've tried harder, done more of the right work to stay in touch,
But know, it's the natural way; we move on, let go of our pasts; even of those who mattered once to us

Ron's still on 13th Street, living his program (I believe),
Ryn's still in Tucson, asking her weird-ass culture questions on Facebook ('cause Art Lives!),
Judy's moved back to the City; I don't know where, but can guess why,
Mary's moved, too; I need to make that call, make that effort to re-connect,
Saw Parand at Supplier's Day; nervously busy, extremely successful;
And I'll include Nancy in here too, writer of cosmetics, longtime East Villager, soon leaving for Mexico
All fade; everything fades. It's natural, to try to hold on; sometimes we can, for a while

My May-birthday friends, each still unknown to each other. your only connection, the poet at the hub,
Wish each of you wonderful days, though the wishes are belated now; the late poet does what he can.
Alone in sweet Wilmington, health slowly weakening, sadness slowly growing, age;
Wish for joy, for good, for each; still strong, still ringing, loudly. Distant friends; alone, I embrace all.

Wilmington, DE
May – June 2013

286.

(287) On Being at EMD for 15 Years

When I was a kid, I wanted to be a white-coat chemist, red & green beakers bubbling on the bench;
Never sure what I was doing at that bench, but I always liked that image.
When I hit graduate school, I looked for pleasure, learned well the bars of New Orleans,
But should've found a neurochemical lab, should've followed the deeper bliss, not just the surface.

As the working man, the son of the working man, often it was about just getting the job,
Just making a living   Learning cleaners and surfactants, color in that hot stamping foil shop,
Lipsticks on the West Coast, ultrasonics in New Jersey. And mostly I didn't like those jobs,
'Cause I longed for DNA research, for cancer breakthroughs—and here I was, with more red lipsticks.

I came to EMD after being let go by the family company, semiconductor fluids; they weren't selling,
And I was gone. Larry called it the *"Talk Show Circuit,"* the resumes, the headhunters, the interviews,
The shaking hands of getting the job; I began. Red lipsticks. Only now I'm grateful, it's almost fun,
And be a part of this industry. Watch the fashion trends. Note the colors. A multinational trip, this is.

So there are German colleagues, and Brazilian, and Chinese, discussing our work via e-mail;
So much I might've done differently, so many mistakes, but it's here. Now. 15 years: it's a good start.

Philadelphia PA
September 2013

287.

(288) Night at Mark and Gregory's

An easy meeting at Panera Bread, a gentle dinner for three,
A ten-minute ride to the house, surrounded by many others,
(And some are new and some are old and somehow it seems to matter, here)

The house is warm and spacious enough, framed paintings, the necessary cable and computer,
Piles of fat art books, medical books, the Norton Anthology of Poetry, Be Here Now,
A tight row of DVDs in the guest room; the well-used, battered Big Book, alive in their bedroom.

They both work early and I stayed up to watch tv, went to bed before 11, read of Ginsberg in India,
Slept finally, dream of having wallet stolen. Checking its usual place, finding two thin twenties,
But it's only a dream; the wallet, in its normal place, shows funds at the ready, the long drive home.

Slept in, woke at 8:40, out of bed by 10:10 – delicious gift!
Showered (watched by sleeping corgi), dressed, packed, taste of sweet coffee cake,
Sweeter raspberry tea: breakfast. I'll call Mark, he'll deliver me out of town.

Things are nice but this is not about things, it's beyond things;
Two married men – two husbands, each to each other,
They begin again. Cold upstate New York. Sure. Why not.

Now, again, the winter highways: on the road, again. Progress; toward home.

Plattsburgh NY – Wilmington, DE
November 2013 – January 2014

288.

(289) Poem Starting With a Line by David Yezzi

for David Silver

There are days I don't think about the sea;

But I think of David on his 9th floor perch, the ruined boardwalk, yet to be concretized,
The empty spaces which were handball courts, stone monoliths still standing,
The spit of sand, wind-blown, eroding, a quarter-mile from the invisible boardwalk to tide's edge;
I call him up and ask how the ocean is, and it's always beautiful, stretching to Africa, to Europe.

To look out upon that ocean is to be humbled, connected, muscular in spirit, joined with the One;
That's his view from the 9th floor, Shore Front Parkway. David, alone with his ocean.

Philadelphia, PA
January 2014

289.

(290) Poem Beginning with a Line by Gertrude Stein

What is a nail. A nail is unison.

That there is form and content
Always believing form grew out of content

Questioning who I am   how I write   what do I do   what do I mean I mean meaning is not a lie
Then what is a lie—a lying whitefoot or a truthful blackfoot
Logic seems overrated   a construct of meaning   of trying to find meaning   of trying to make meaning
Meaning out of a toybox   a word jungle   a website of all that purports to be true

Meaning is an orange tree in the middle of a February frost
Meaning is black snow burning an Atlanta highway
Meaning is oil slicks, rainbow colors disco Studio 54
Meaning is a black & white photo of Mailer & Capote drunk off their asses
Meaning is Philip Seymour Hoffman dying with a needle in his arm
Meaning is not what we think   it's not what we want it to be   it's not the hotspots at the ocean's floor
Meaning is that truth which we hope the autopsy will discover
Meaning may be overrated as well

That's not what I mean   that's not what I meant   it has nothing to do with who I am
With how I sound or look or think or act or drive or kiss or cry cry cry
No self-pity here   there's no room for it   no time for it   no one here to laugh back
Deeper and deeper. Deeper.

Darker than within the rings of the redwoods
Darker than the mineshafts, the living walls, the black bats
Darker than the depths of sand, the ocean floor,
Darker than the living burial, the shoveled dirt catching the eyes, the throat
Darker. Deeper.   Darker. Deeper.

"...a tale told by an idiot, full of sound and fury, signifying nothing."

But maybe not.

Wilmington, DE/February 2014

290.

(291) Cover Letter

Bright clear Sunday afternoon here in DE, doing laundry, thinking of friends;
Enclosing a set of new (-ish) poems, along with the first real book in the world,
Available on Amazon, but now you've got your copy, along with my recent thinking;
7 am tomorrow I report to the 7th floor, Wilmington Hospital, where the surgeon will
    Remove the malfunctioning knee, replace it with titanium and plastic;
    Looking forward to slow, gentle healing; and three months away from the job.

Been meaning to send the book out to you, but laziness & life interfere;
The poems are improving, mood's better now than the self-created miseries, last year.
It's not much, I know, I want so to write more, and better (always, better),
But the words are always just a reflection of the heart, of the spirit, sometimes struggling;
    Want them at least to be honest, authentic, real, who I am, what I'm doing, here, now;
    Since here & now always changes, the poems do as well. This life; this continuing change.

In the rooms, I've been quoting Harpo Marx: *"No matter how bad the show, 11:00 always comes."*
Another step in the unfolding: one man's small life. Next steps include pain, and healing. It'll be OK.

Wilmington, DE
February 2014

291.

(292) Knee Replacement/PT Poem
for Michele

Into the hospital, 24 February: total knee replacement, left knee. Bedridden, four interesting days,
Then into rehab, a holding, healing place; 17 days. The thick, six-inch scar, some weeping of blood;
Some recovery. I moved from a wheelchair to a walker, was given a walker on the day that I left;
Back home in the basement apartment, the first thing was to put it away.   I need to walk,

To practice stairs. Up is fine, but down causes sharp pain, the bending, the back of the knee;
The fighting through it. Accept: this is the test, the need, the work that's now before me.
Very fortunate: insurance's approval. Evaluation at surgeon's, at PT, okay for six weeks, thrice weekly.
The surgical leg bloated, heavily swollen; thickened tissues resisting movement. I began in the pool.

For three weeks I was lowered into warm chlorinated water, suspended, buoyant, tethered, impelling
The thick left leg through four timed minutes of each: walking, marching, scissors, butt kicks, skiing.
Then stretching the muscles, the back of the knee. And Michele's massage, manipulation, pushing
Into the burn of a measurement: angle of movement, 80 to 110. Five weeks. This stuff does work.

Approaching the end, this practice, expect to go back to work mid-May; need to work on attitude;
Surgery's OK, the slowly-slimming leg, PT's OK, functional progress. Recovering; consciously.

Wilmington, DE
April 2014

(293) Saturday Afternoon 4/5/2014

It's still the thickness of my left leg, the thigh especially,
the trauma-recovering; the knee replacement

There is silence now, though the silence is not pure—a breathing, I suppose,
the heat pulled up to 77, a gentle hum but no, it is not silence

It is as silent as I get in this world, this world I create, my own making, my own doing

Usually there's music. Earlier an old tape, Dave Mason's Greatest Hits,
which I bought so that I'd own *"We Just Disagree;"* for Mary, but more, for me

I think of the friends I've lost, Mary, Rick, Ron, even David, who rarely calls nowadays
And when I call it's a hurried conversation, an *"I did this, you did that, I'm feeling old & tired"*

Choosing to remain alone

Now there is silence. Let these words enter the silence

It is little. It is a small thing that I do. But I wish to continue:
The ivy covering the bare wooded trunk. Green buds still cowering from the chill.

Saturday. The day not yet spent; the day not yet wasted.

Wilmington, DE
April 2014

293.

(294) Haircut

Almost cut my hair, it happened just the other day.
It was gettin' kinda long, could've said it was in my way.
But I didn't and I wonder why. Feel like letting my freak flag fly,
'Cause I feel like I owe it...to someone.
                                        —David Crosby

I'd tried growing my gray hair longer & longer, my passive aggression, my freak flag flying,
But it'd became an annoyance, thick strands of rich keratin flying off at odd angles, unkempt,
Glancing in a mirror, especially driving, out of control, wonder at the impression I'm giving;
It's only hair; I'm the one attributing more to it. It's only hair. And maybe it is.

The parking lot surprisingly filled, but in the shop only two guys, Zach, blonde, late 20's,
Football-player build, in the franchise uniform of black shirt & pants, just finishing up a redheaded kid.
Johnny Cash on the speaker, just a voice & guitar: *"Don't forget to give my love to Rose;"*
Later, check You-tube for lyrics, click on to his *Drive on, it don't mean nothin', drive on.* Yeah.

In the old days, NYC, I'd go to Sigfridio's on First Avenue; always waited for Bruno,
Thick black mustache, ever-increasing widow's peak; knew me well enough, knew me without asking.
The old-time barber shop, a man's refuge, I read Esquire and perused GQ while I waited.
Today Keith came out of the back, invited me to the chair. Finally, I was ready.

Thick clipped gray on the black smock, careful the clippers, the beard, around the ears; just a
Simple haircut, but look & feel different. Freak flag's underground, now. Don't mean it's not here.

Wilmington. DE
August 2014

294.

(295) Poem for David

Moving slower, now
There's a chair in the shower
But I put on Jay McShann's big band from the pile of CD's
And the ever-changing, ever-constant ocean, still just across the street, your 9th floor glorious view

Drove through car-jammed Queens yesterday, got off the solid Van Wyck, tried the Jackie Robinson;
Crowded too, but it broke soon, Myrtle Ave to Woodhaven to Cross Bay to Rockaway
$3.75 toll at the bridge! Was 15¢ when I moved here, more than 50 years ago, now
I pay with a Lincoln, the E-Z Pass still on my desk, still waiting to be renewed

The refrigerator needs a little help, a tiny stepstool, to stay closed.
I finish your gallon of sweet iced tea, open another,
Think you might have some difficulty, opening the cap;
Physically you're weaker now, slower to move. Then again, you've never been 84 before.

Perfect big band, perfect near-empty beach, perfect ocean,
Perfect sky, pale blue softened now by perfect oncoming cloud cover
I'll head back to my car with a buttered roll, iced coffee and a parking ticket--street cleaning.
Cursing the tolls, Marine Park, Verrazano, Turnpike, Delaware Bridge--that E-Z Pass, still on my desk.

Maybe I'll come back here to live, Rockaway, my last apartment across from the ocean
My mother's last apartment; maybe yours, too.
I brought up Death, 'cause he seemed present here, your hang-dog face, the old Irish ladies around
You don't fear it, but don't want it to hurt. Don't want it to hurt your ex-wife, your current child.

The end of the ride, 900 miles in less than a week; Easton, Gregory, David, Rockaway.
I wished for more internal change. Monday, the job, again. By Friday, the depression's real.
Highway miles, local radio stations, friends of years and friends newly met;
The silent apartment, broken by bits of jazz and ball games. 9th floor; the ocean, across.

Wilmington, DE
September - October 2014

295.

(296) Engender: the desert work, the clarity of the rain

after Marianne Boruch

I do the desert work, know the clarity of the rain.
Questioning, always: subtleties, grief, terror, now close friends.
No longer bothering, the fight: accepting.
Moving through; moving past. The bright new apple of

This green day; the silent parking lot. Waiting. It is, all is,
All are; the separation of appearances; growth.
To be present, watchful, cognizant of the multitude, all their
Changes. The speeding panel truck, the 4 x 4. Trumpet: iPod jazz.

Knowing this could be anywhere, Lyon, Kabul, the dusty foot-printed
Craters of Mars, of moon, we search for a path,
Direction, want so to avoid the quicksand, the baited
Traps we've made for others; we fear the hunter's capture. Wait. Stop.

"It may be a prayer, or it may only be a poem." True
Enough, yet even these small things may have real power. Moods may yet shift.
The desert may yet offer its unique compassion; the singing clarity of the rain
May yet be ours. This is a fragment, complete in itself:
      building, as on a keystone. The gentleness; the light.

Lewes, DE
October 2014

(297) After Whitman's "A Clear Midnight"

After all the hours, allowing the warmth of silence, the comfort of darkness,
Beyond which had been tempted, tried, the planning of business, the speedy burning gasoline,
She waits for me, calls to me. It's in that dream-time her separate reality is offered.

Hers a truth, even unseen, unknown, in the brutal light, the pitiless life of day.

Not yet wise enough to grasp her meanings. Anchored in appearance, tied to data, to facts,
Knowing the existence of worlds valid as dawn, shrouded, dark, inaccessible, but to the knowers.
To undertake this journey, to trust in all that waits, in all that will be revealed; moving.

Into the experience. Into this experience.

Wilmington, DE
March 2015

(298) After: The Hudson at China Point

Once in midwinter saw the image of the pier deep in drifted snow

    The river a deep gray the sky three levels lighter, gray upon gray,
    The smokestack giving forth gray upon gray upon gray

    The sound of water lapping wooden pier, the train flying toward the City
    The sounds shrouded in the comforting ease of natural winter silence

    The reasons I return, returning now, as the basement window gives the caution of early spring,
    The reasons I love to return, must return, the quiet, centering place, allowing for deep breath,

    The challenges still here for me, the imperfections, body mind spirit intellect, soul-work,
    The needed soul-work dangling before me, the visions available, only for me to do this work

    The work done with eyes closed, body calmed, vision sharper than imagination,
    The visions, the beyond-ordinary reality, where I meet my animals of power, teachers of this art

    The worlds beginning to access, the teachings being offered to me, all I need is to ask, to do;
    The reasons for these gifts, healing, strength, making myself useful, power building on power

Early spring, into Jersey, again. Again, I enter the circle; histories alive, futures, shining within me.

Wilmington DE
April 2015

Biographical Statement

Phil Linz was born in Brooklyn, NY, and was raised in the Rockaway Beach section of Queens, NY. He has also lived in New Orleans, Tucson, Los Angeles, New York City (East Village), Morrisville, PA, Croton-on-Hudson, NY, and Pooler, GA; since October 2011 he has lived in Wilmington, DE. After almost 40 years as a working chemist, Mr. Linz retired in May, 2018.

He's been writing poetry since 1971 and is the founder and publisher of Fierce Grace Press, specializing in chapbooks, believing in the concept of *"Publishing Under the Radar."*

This volume includes his eight published chapbooks and two unpublished collections.

Mr. Linz may be reached at *linzp18@verizon.net*.

www.ingramcontent.com/pod-product-compliance
Lightning Source LLC
Chambersburg PA
CBHW080325270326
41927CB00014B/3105